The MacLenose Trail

By Richard Peace

Photographs by David Bottomley and Kaarlo Schepel

Includes 4 excursions joining/crossing the Trail
by Kaarlo Schepel

The Alternative Press
P.O. Box 47141, Morrison Hill
Hong Kong
Fax: (852) 2890 2186
Telephone: 2577 6319

The MacLehose Trail

First Edition, August 1995

Published by The Alternative Press
P.O. Box 47141, Morrison Hill, Hong Kong

Edited by Lesley Logan

Cover design by Jojo Design Studio Ltd

Original drawings/maps by Rachel Walker and the author

This book is sold subject to the condition that it will not, by way of trade or otherwise, be lent, re-sold, hired out, or circulated without the publisher's prior consent, except for short quotations in reviews. All rights reserved.

Printed and bound in Hong Kong

The MacLehose Trail

Contents

Section	Footprint	Page
	FOREWORD	4
	INTRODUCTION	6
1	Pak Tam Chung to Long Ke Beach	15
2	Long Ke Beach to Pak Tam Au	23
3	Pak Tam Au to Kei Ling Ha	36
Ex 1	*Sai Kung to Kwong Yuen Estate*	45
4	Kei Ling Ha to Tate's Cairn	51
5	Tate's Cairn to Tai Po Road	60
Ex 2	*Tai Wai to Tsuen Wan*	73
6	Tai Po Road to Shing Mun Reservoir	79
7	Shing Mun Reservoir to Lead Mine Pass	86
Ex 3	*Fo Tan Station to Grassy Hill*	97
8	Lead Mine Pass to Route Twisk	105
9	Route Twisk to Tin Fu Tsai	113
10	Tin Fu Tsai to Tuen Mun	121
Ex 4	*Tsing Lung Tau to Sham Tseng*	128

Appendix	Maps & Charts	
A	Route Profiles (elevation)	135
B	Route Maps (with Introduction)	147
C	*Excursions*	175

Foreword

This book is a real guide to the Trail and I hope it will encourage people to use and enjoy it.

Those already familiar with walking it will find additional interest by its references to scenes and villages through which it passes; to those not so familiar it offers invaluable guidance on what to expect; on what sections are physically demanding and those which are not, and how to get to and from them without being committed to walking the Trail's formidable full length. It also alerts walkers to what to expect scenically and from what places to look out for the most attractive views.

The Trail was laid out to draw attention to the rural variety and beauty of the country parks and to encourage people to enjoy them and so to preserve them. I feel sure this book will assist these purposes.

Lord MacLehose of Beoch
Beoch, Maybole
Ayrshire, KA19 8EN
(7th February, 1995)

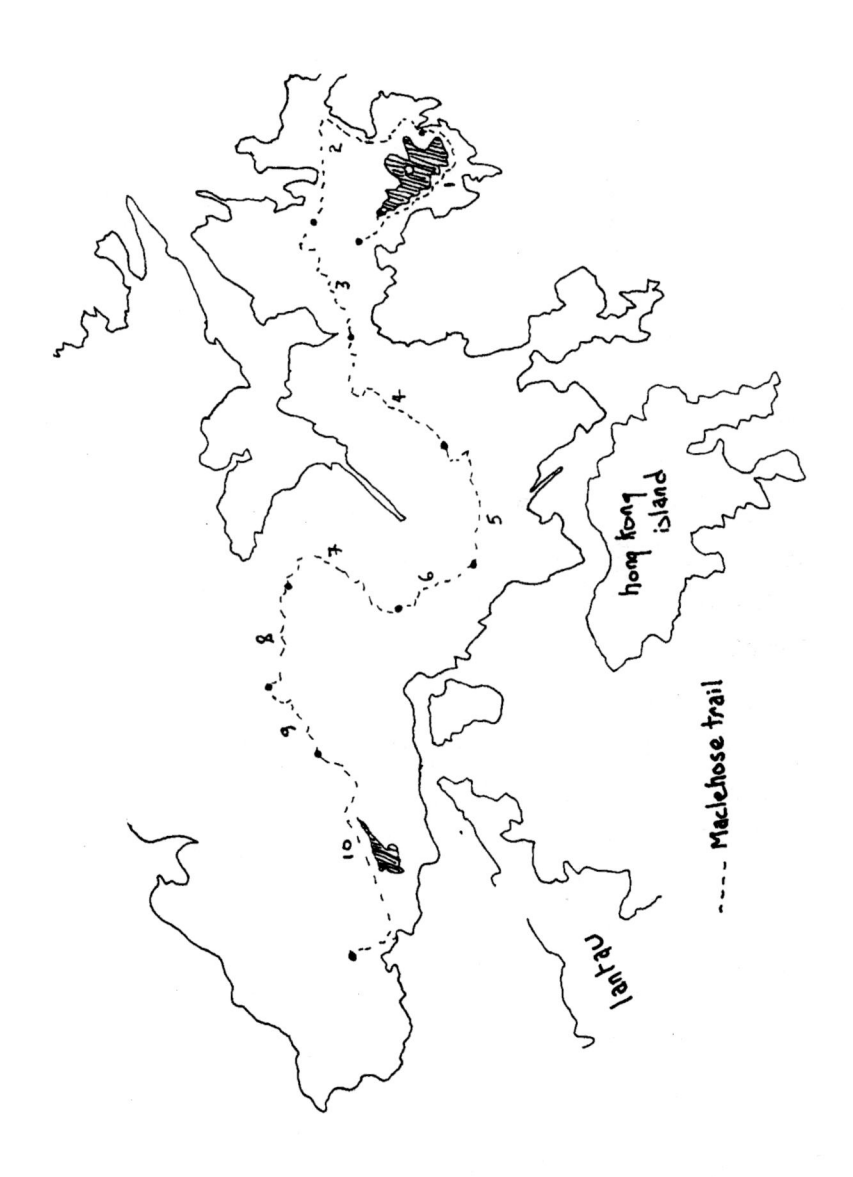

The MacLehose Trail

The MacLehose Trail

Introduction

The Route

Hong Kong is often thought of as a glittering city – frequently compared to a pearl, due to its grandeur and lustre, as well as its proximity to the Chinese Pearl River. However, many tourists and long-time residents of Hong Kong are surprised to learn of the easily accessible and abundant variety of countryside within Hong Kong's borders in the New Territories, just to the north of the bustling metropolis. The long distance walking trail known as the MacLehose Trail, stretching the length of the New Territories from east to west, allows both local resident and visitor to witness relatively little-known but beautiful aspects of Hong Kong. The route can be considered as a number of day walks or as a challenging whole. The majority of the sections are easily accessible by public transport so you can be flexible in the amount of time you spend hiking, whether you have a day or a couple of weeks.

From the contrasting white beaches of east Sai Kung to the high peaks of Ma On Shan, from traditional rural villages to superb vistas of modern Hong Kong – all these are right on the city's doorstep in the New Territories. The trail is generally very well worn which is not surprising as the annual Trailwalkers Charity Walk, whose aim is to cover the trail in under 24 hours, may consist of hundreds of teams of four people! As long as you follow the general safety hints below, you shouldn't encounter any difficulties. You'll find what you're looking for, be it fun and excitement or quiet relaxation.

Named after a former governor of Hong Kong, Sir Murray MacLehose (1971-1982), the trail reflects both his love of the outdoors and his desire for others to share this enthusiasm. He was also instrumental in expanding the country parks which originated in the 1970s, many of which the trail goes through. His spirit lives on in the parks' encouragement of the preservation of

The MacLehose Trail

Hong Kong's countryside and the enjoyment of it by her population, in a peaceful and responsible manner. It was clearly his wish that conservation, education and pleasure should go hand in hand. This guide will hopefully encourage that ethos in others. With over 70 % of Hong Kong's 1045 square kilometres being natural countryside, it seems tragic that so few people are aware of the acres of natural beauty in their own backyard (although it must be admitted that green space in Hong Kong is constantly dwindling and will probably have decreased further by the time you read this book; all the more reason to preserve and enjoy it). We can only hope that the worst of the relentless development of this once rural area is over. The country parks are a major obstacle to such development. 40% of Hong Kong's total area is made up of designated country parks and building in these areas is strictly controlled by ordinance.

This guide splits the route into ten sections. Each section may be tackled by a fit person, and two or more sections can be combined on a camping holiday. For the fit and well-equipped, I'd advise a long holiday to hike the whole trail in one go ! The trail is graded one to three in order of ascending difficulty. Profiles are also given for comparative purposes: grade three sections may look difficult but the horizontal scale is restricted because of space, so don't be scared by the steep-looking gradients on these maps. They are not quite as bad as they appear. You can see at a glance which are the hard sections and which are easy sections. Whatever your level of fitness, there's an appropriate trail section for you. Grade one trails are for first time walkers or those who don't wish to push themselves at all physically, whilst grade two walkers should preferably have some experience of grade one trails. A reasonable level of fitness and some prior experience is definitely necessary for grade three sections. Although they may have similar lengths, the grade three sections are physically quite punishing and you may find yourself going very slowly or coming to a halt on some of the steeper climbs if you don't have a basic level of fitness, especially in the summer months.

There's no need to stick religiously to the routes suggested. 'Escape Routes' are marked in the text which allow you to split off from the trail should the weather become bad or if you wish to cut your journey short for any reason. The extra routes can be used for access to the trail or are walks in themselves.

What To Take

Essentials

* A good waterproof backpack big enough to take the items below. Small 'day packs' can be purchased for shorter trips or larger backpacks for those who want to try camping or even the whole trail.

* A large scale map. At least 1:25,000. See the note on maps below. You may want to buy the plastic-covered versions of these or at least put your map in a clear transparent bag and seal it to protect it from rain.

* A good compass. Practice using it to chart your direction on a map. This is especially important on the few places of the trail where the path may become indistinct. It will also help reassure you, when in the middle of a long section, that your direction is correct. (See notes on using a compass below). Ninety per cent of the trail is so well-marked you shouldn't need the aid of this device, but occasionally the trail becomes unclear or thick fog rolls in , so always take a compass – even if only used once in a hundred trips, it could get you out of a tricky situation.

*Suitable clothing to include:

Stout footwear with a good grip. Trainers are fine for sections graded one and two, but for grade three sections stout hiking boots with a good grip are recommended as these sections may involve scrambling over rocks and, in the rain, wet clay-like soil.

Generally light clothing, unless going in the winter months

of December - February when a second layer may be advisable. Also take a light waterproof in the winter months. Getting wet in the rainy season may be uncomfortable but the weather is not cold enough for it to become a real problem.

Shade is vital if you are hiking the trail on a sunny day in the summer months. A brimmed white hat is best, or even an umbrella if it's not too windy. Without shade, the summer sun is extremely punishing. I recall foolishly doing one of the sections without any kind of shade. I suffered several days of pain and numerous jokes about my head's bright red appearance. Heatstroke is a much more serious problem you shouldn't risk.

* Water is vital, especially in the summer months. The main danger for walkers in Hong Kong's climate is dehydration. Drink often. A water bottle is a good idea which will allow you to take a quick swig whilst on the move.

* Food – take plenty of juicy fruit and convenient snack food such as sandwiches. This is especially important if you are attempting more than one part of the trail over a number of days.

* Basic first aid kit to include bandages, plaster and disinfectant.

* A torch or flashlight which can be used in emergency situations.

* Even in winter, mosquito repellent will save you a lot of scratching.

Optional Extras That May Be Useful

* Sunglasses.

* Camera. Beware of taking one in the rainy season as damp or rain may affect its performance. It's best to take some sort of cover or plastic bag to protect it from the elements.

* Sun lotion. The hot summer sun can easily burn you badly within an hour if you have sensitive skin, and the thinning ozone

layer makes the sun a hazard even for dark skin.

* A small lightweight pair of binoculars. Useful for looking at ships or birds or identifying distant objects.

Safety

Follow these safety tips carefully and you'll have an enjoyable and safe trip:

* Know your own physical limits. If inexperienced, start on one of the grade one sections. If concerned about any aspect of your health, consult your physician before you undertake a hiking trip.

* If inexperienced, do not go alone. A friend will be able to get help if necessary. There is always 'safety in numbers'

* Get a map of the area and learn to use it. Study it beforehand and make a note of the major landmarks you will pass.

* Do not walk into hills shrouded in mist or fog. It is very easy to get lost when you have no landmarks or can't see the trail ahead to guide you. It is better to turn back and retrace your footsteps than to proceed into difficult conditions. There may be an escape route to a nearby road over low ground. Always give yourself spare time to complete the walk to allow for such contingencies as bad weather.

*Know the weather forecast for the duration of your walk. If in doubt about weather conditions, it's always safer to cancel your trip than get caught in very bad weather. This is especially obvious when a typhoon is in Hong Kong's vicinity.

* Someone at home should know exactly where you are going and by what time you should have returned. If you don't return this will allow the correct area to be searched.

* Do not enter water tunnels or catch waters. They can flood extremely quickly and can easily drown a person.

* Do not continue on minor paths when they appear to be

overgrown or petering out – you could be walking down a dead-end or impassable path. This should not be the case on any of the MacLehose Trail, which has all the hallmarks of a well-used long distance footpath. Most of it is very well worn and the trail can often be seen leading over the hills in front of you. It is also signposted and way marked by a hiker figure or yellow arrow or yellow spray painted dots at important junctions. There's the occasional place where direction choice may be difficult or the path narrow, but these have been detailed in the text.

* When taking drinking water from mountain streams, ensure the stream is not fed by inhabited or cultivated areas that may pollute it. Water sterilization tablets are a good idea if your trip is so long that you'll need to drink stream water.

How To Take A Compass Bearing

This is simple with practice and should become a habit. Use in conjunction with a map. These instructions are based on a simple design needle compass.

1. Place the long edge of the compass along the path you wish to follow on the map – although the path may vary a little it will have a general direction.

2. Turn the central capsule until the N/S lines of the capsule match the northern grid lines on the map.

3. Hold the compass and map and turn around until the north needle is parallel with the grid lines and pointing north.

4. The long edge of your compass will now tell you where to go.

5. To cut down on use of the compass, when you ascertain your general direction make a mental note of those objects you should aim for: a hill, a radio mast or a village, for example.

6. If you have any doubts about where you are, use the compass. Don't leave it until you have made several guesses and are

completely lost.

7. If you have the extremely simple circular watch type compass, with no rotating capsule, place it on your present location on the map. Turn around until the north needle is in line with the north gridlines. You are now pointing north so consult the map to find your desired direction of travel.

Trailwalker

Trailwalker is an annual charity walk held every autumn over the length of the MacLehose Trail. Teams of four set out to cover the 100km in under 48hrs to raise money for charity. Since 1981, Trailwalker has raised over $45 m for the disabled in Hong Kong, to build schools and give medical services in Nepal, and to support Oxfam Hong Kong's work with the poor in Asia and Africa. Over 2000 take part and, while you are unlikely to beat the Gurkha's record of 13 hrs 18 min, the special atmosphere and sense of achievement as you stagger across the finishing line, make it an unforgettable experience for even the slowest walkers.

A Word About Maps

You should find the directions and maps in this book perfectly adequate for the majority of the trail. If you do happen to lose the trail or become lost in fog, then maps and a compass are invaluable. You are strongly advised to take the relevant map and compass, even though you may not need it 99% of the time.

There are a variety of maps available, detailed below, but it's important that it be at least 1:25,000 scale. All should be available from the Government Publications Centre (2523 1910) near Admiralty (see next page) or the Hong Kong Tourist Association Office in the basement of Jardine House (8 am - 6pm 2801 7177).

a. The series of maps entitled HM20C, published by the Hong Kong Government, are the best and most accurate maps for walking and show many important features with a clear brightly-coloured key. They cost about $30.00 each from the Government Publications Centre on the Ground Floor of the Government Of-

The MacLehose Trail

fices (Low Block) on Queensway (opposite Admiralty Station). There are 16 in the whole series, but the pertinent ones are as follows:

MacLehose Trail Section	Map Sheet no.
1,2,3.	8
4	7 and 8
5	7 and 11
6	7 and 11
7	7
8	6 and 7
9	6
10	6

The only drawback is that they don't have the trail marked on them. I managed to use these maps together with the Country Parks maps (see c. below).

Beware if you decide to take a detour from the MacLehose Trail down a footpath marked on this series of maps. Although they show numerous footpaths, many of these are overgrown to the point of extinction. Always make a careful note of the way you have come so retracing your footsteps is not necessary. These maps differ markedly in respect to English maps which usually show well-established paths, easily found. Of course England doesn't have the tropical summer and fast-growing vegetation which can quickly obscure even well-used footpaths in Hong Kong.

b. The Countryside series of maps published by the Government Printer (1:25,000) are also very highly recommended and are the easiest and cheapest option, especially for those intending to hike more than one stage of the trail. They show the topography of the area very clearly and are designed for walkers, showing such features as the MacLehose Trail (amongst other designated trails), campsites and points of local and historical interest. Three maps cover the whole trail:

* Sai Kung and Clearwater Bay.
* Central New Territories.
* North West New Territories.

They cost $25.00 each

c. Country Parks Authority have maps specifically of the trail itself – a generic one as well as one of each section. However, being in black and white it's difficult to distinguish the different features and figure out exactly where the trail goes.

d. The Hong Kong Guidebook by Universal Publications shows all urban areas in detail including numbered bus routes, and may be useful for those less familiar with the layout of Hong Kong and its public transport. It's available from major book shops.

A Note On Place Names

Chinese place names can be confusing and repetitive even for those who have some familiarity with Cantonese. It makes it a lot easier to identify topography if you can remember the following basic terms:

shan: hill or mountain (Ngau Yee Shek Shan = Cow's Ear Hill)

sai: usually means west (Sai Wan = West Bay)

wan: usually means bay

shek: rock or stone, often applied to smaller or rocky hills (Lui Ta Shek = Lightning Strikes Rock)

au: pass or valley (Chui Tung Au is the flat area at the bottom of the valley on Section Two as you approach Sai Wan Beach)

* * * *

The MacLehose Trail

Section 1
Pak Tam Chung to Long Ke Beach
Difficulty: Grade 1. Time Estimate : 3-4 hours; 10.6 km

The road that makes up most of this trail, bordered by the silent depths of High Island Reservoir on one side and the South China Sea on the other, was completely deserted when I hiked it on a hot summer's day. The prize at the end of 10km is a white, sweeping beach, with a good view of Sai Kung. Sections Two and Three take you over some of the higher peaks in this area which is the last large chunk of Hong Kong that is still relatively undeveloped.

It's great for beginners as it's one of the easier sections. Ninety percent of it is on tarmac road with only three moderate climbs, the first one up a long incline from Pak Tam Chung . The second is a climb and drop over a couple of kilometres in the middle of the route leading towards the viewpoint over Rocky Harbour.

Turn right for Man Yee Road and Long Ke

Finally, the steepest incline comes as you climb over a small peninsula at the eastern dam and drop down to Long Ke Wan. Otherwise the road remains fairly level. It would serve as a good testing ground for those who are apprehensive about the harder sections of the trail and who want to gauge their fitness and ability. It wouldn't stretch an experienced hiker who might find it unchallenging.

However, if you don't want to scramble up hillsides or zigzag your way down river valleys, but just want quiet, pleasant scenery and a fine beach, this walk is perfect. If you find this section extremely difficult it's probably smart to hike the other Grade One sections until you become more confident in your ability to move onto Sections Two and Three.

A good idea might be to take a taxi to the eastern dam and climb the last part over the rough track to the beach. You can spend a good part of the day swimming and relaxing on the beach and then take a pleasant walk back to Pak Tam Chung to get a bus. If you decide to walk out to Long Ke you might not be able to find a taxi and may have to try your luck hitch-hiking, as there

Eternal beauty at High Island Reservoir

The MacLehose Trail

Wild life at Pak Tam Chung

is no public transport at the end of the dam. See the Transport Section for details.

An even better alternative would be to do the whole of this section plus Section Two as far as Chui Tung Au, where there's a good escape route down Sai Wan Sai Kung Road (see Section Two for details). This would make the walk about 14 kilometres, without repeating any of the route.

1. ROUTE DETAILS

Pak Tam Chung to Choi Hing Dam

Get off bus #94 at Pak Tam Chung car park. Go onto the main road. Go left (northeast) for half a kilometre over a river to a split in the road. The road passes a soft drink shop on the right. The split is marked by a notice board at the actual start of the MacLehose Trail. Go right at this junction sign posted for High Island Reservoir on Tai Mong Tsai Road. The main road climbs gradually for one kilometre until you come to a mini roundabout. Take the first right onto Sai Kung Man Yee Road. Ignore the first

The MacLehose Trail

The main dam overlooking High Island Reservoir and Sai Kung

left on Sai Kung Man Yee Road, a rough dirt track. Continue on for about two more kilometres through sparsely wooded country skirting the edge of the reservoir. A campsite is marked on the right down an unpaved road. Ignore this. Go across a small dam on the right and past a police post above you on the right, then cross a large dam. On your right is Chong Hing Water Sports Centre and behind that are the huts of High Island Detention Centre. There are spectacular views of the hill ranges behind the detention centre from here, with Urn Island and Kau Sai Chau Island in the foreground.

Choi Hing to Eastern Dam

After the dam the road climbs gradually for about a kilometre to a viewpoint looking south from High Island. There's a worn metal plaque showing the main landmarks as you look out over a spectacular view of Rocky Harbour, which can be glimpsed through the trees. The road descends for another two and a half kilometres and reemerges near eastern dam. Wonderful views of Sharp Peak can be seen to the north. Cross over the eastern end of the dam wall after passing the large blue monument to those who died in the construction of the High Island Reservoir Project.

The MacLehose Trail

Eastern Dam to Long Ke Beach

At the far end of the dam a very rough, wide stone track ascends round a corner. At the top go straight across. The steps on the right lead to a small shelter. The track becomes narrow on the descent to Long Ke Beach, which can be seen from the path. There are two splits in the path. Go right at both. There's a trail information board at the first split and both routes are marked by a yellow arrow. The path turns right in front of the gates to the Wui Oi Monastery at the back of the beach and follows a sand track behind the beach. Overnighters will be interested in the campsite at the back of the beach.

2. NATURAL FEATURES AND HISTORY

The most notable feature of the Sai Kung peninsula (with the exception of Sharp Peak in the north) is the green rounded bunches of volcanic rock that drop down to the sea. In places, as at Long Ke, needle-like strata are visible where the sea has worn away the natural vegetation. More of the natural history of the area can

The waterfront in Sai Kung

be seen at the Pak Tam Chung Visitor Centre next to the bus stop.

The massive High Island Reservoir Project was officially opened in November 1979. The reservoir was once a sea bay, with fisherman living along its banks. The local families were compensated for their land and relocated to housing estates by the government. After the dams were build, the sea water was pumped out and the dam was filled with fresh water. High Island is second only to Plover Cove rReservoir in size yet most of Hong Kong's fresh water supply is still pumped from China. The eastern coffer dam is the largest of its kind in the world - it needs to be to keep the South China Sea at bay. The whole project cost a staggering HK$1348 million. The reservoir resembles a huge empty lake; you can best appreciate the massive amount of manpower that must have gone into the project by looking out over the eastern dam onto this huge barricade against the Pacific.

Looking over Choi Hing, the islands of Kai Sai Chau and Sharp Island rise one behind another. These islands are sparsely inhabited but the area is popular with boaters and water sports enthusiasts, especially at weekends. This may soon change as permission has just been given to build a public golf course - the first in Hong Kong - on Kai Sau Island. The later view over Rocky Harbour is the one of the best on this part of the trail, and I noticed it was quite popular with couples in cars who no doubt come to admire the scenery. You can see rocky bays and quiet inaccessible harbours neatly framed by a canopy of trees. It's hard to imagine civilisation is only a few kilometres away.

Living History At High Island Reservoir.

Chong Hing Detention Centre

The Chong Hing Detention Centre, which can be viewed as you pass over the first dam on the southern side of the reservoir, houses Vietnamese boat people. These unfortunate souls first started arriving in Hong Kong after the fall of Saigon to the North Vietnamese Communist forces in 1975.

The closed camp system as seen at Chong Hing was instituted in 1982 by the government and was part of the policy of so-called 'humane deterrence' that was designed to discourage more boat people from fleeing to Hong Kong. Chong Hing itself was opened in 1989 over much local protest. The question remains of what will happen to these people and their camp-born children in 1997 when Hong Kong is handed over to the People's Republic of China. Beijing has insisted that all Vietnamese in detention camps must be repatriated before the 1997 handover, and that process has been started amid great controversy.

3. TRANSPORT AND OTHER DETAILS.
Getting There.

The main access point to the Sai Kung and Ma On Shan Country Parks is from Choi Hung, the MTR stop in the middle of the Kwun Tong line. Take exit B which brings you out onto the main road with the bus terminal in front of you. On the other side are buses serving Kowloon and the drop off point if you return to the MTR on bus #94.

From Choi Hung MTR station take bus #92 or the green minibus #1 to Sai Kung, a twenty minute ride. Get off at the terminus in Sai Kung, which has separate stations for the minibuses and the major public and KMB buses. Take bus #94 to Pak Tam Chung (final destination Wong Shek Pier). Pak Tam Chung is after the village of Tai Mong Tsai and you will stop next to the car park and opposite a holiday centre. It's a 15-minute ride. If in doubt you could sit near the front of the bus and ask the driver for Pak Tam Chung as you set off. There's a small drinks and food kiosk where you may stock up, but this seems to open somewhat late in the morning, so don't rely on it if arriving early. Also beware that there are no stores on Section One, even on Long Ke Beach.

Regular buses:

#92 – CHOI HUNG to SAI KUNG: Regularly at 10 min intervals from 6 am to 11 pm. There are also regular minibuses.

#96 – SAI KUNG to WONG SHEK: 7.00 am to 7.00 pm hourly, on the hour.

There is also a bus #96R on Sundays and Public Holidays only that goes from Choi Hung MTR to Wong Shek.

Getting Away

Unless you continue on to Section 2, you have to come back the way you came. For variety, you may want to take a taxi to the end of the beach reservoir and walk back.

There is a service on Section 2 from Sai Wan Sai Kung Road by a private transport operator every half hour, but only on weekends and public holidays. It makes most sense to continue onto Section 2 to this point and get this minibus/truck back from Chui Tung Au to Tai Mong Tsai and then bus #94 to Sai Kung.

Camping Sites And Other Details.

There are four campsites near the routes. By far the most picturesque is the one on Long Ke beach. This can be crowded at weekends as people often tend to come out in large groups.

Of the other three, the first is before you reach the reservoir, the second down the footpath before the Water Sports Centre and the third about half a kilometre before the eastern dam.

* * * *

The MacLehose Trail

Section 2
Long Ke Beach to Pak Tam Au
Difficulty: GRADE 2. Time Estimate: 5-6 Hours; 13.5 km

If you want to see the least developed beaches in Hong Kong backed by lush jungle and traditional villages this is the trail for you. It's accessed from Choi Hung and Sai Kung and ends up at a road where you can get the bus back to Sai Kung. There are several good cafes en route which spare you the hassle of making and packing food. It's one of my favourite sections of the trail and is unique in its scenery.

This section starts off with a steep, long, winding climb, the hardest part of the whole trail up the 314m Sai Wan Shan. You can then take in four of the most beautiful beaches in Hong Kong. There are only a couple of moderate climbs before and after Chek Keng, the small village on the eastern arm of Tolo Harbour. The path is mostly paved. This is a trip to make if you want to see one of the most rural parts of Hong Kong.

Overlooking Tsang Pang Kok Peninsula

The MacLehose Trail

It is, however, a long trip requiring considerable stamina. It's ideal for a two day hike, staying overnight at a campsite, perhaps one after Sai Wan, which would enable you to go at a more leisurely pace.

1. ROUTE DETAILS

Long Ke to Sai Wan Beach

It is quite easy to follow the trail through the rough pine forest at the back of Long Ke. The trail climbs away from the beach at the side of a wooded stream. You get the best views from here of the beautifully cultivated fields of the nearby monastery. The path that winds to the Sai Wan Shan ridge was in the process of being concreted at the time of writing. The path will be even more visible and be less prone to erosion when this paving is completed. However beneficial, the concrete does detract from the feeling that you're in the wilds.

The path twists north and looks like little more than soil erosion in places. There are a couple of

Annual Trailwalker crowd descending from Sai Wan Shan

The MacLehose Trail

Sai Wan Beach with the 1994 trailwalkers (Sharp Peak far left)

climbs interspersed with plateaus. In the upper sections, all of High Island Reservoir stretches out before you and wild valleys and hills on your other side drop steeply to the South China Sea. There is a rough plateau before the final climb to the ridge of Sai Wan Shan. DO NOT go right here - a path splits off to the northeast past an old gate and some barbed wire - this is wrong and will land you down a dead end in the eastern-most part of the peninsula. The path then climbs through pretty shrubs to a point at the summit of Sai Wan Shan. Coming over the summit, four idyllic beaches stretch away to the north with sharp mountain peaks rising majestically in the background.

There are many way markers on the descent, both the hiker figure and yellow spots of paint. Don't worry as the trail first bends west away from the general direction of your destination, Sai Wan Beach. You appear to be walking towards the reservoir and back down the northern side of the dam. You'll see an unusual square-shaped rocky tor sticking up above the dam. Drop down to a ridge with a valley on the left leading to the dam and

The MacLehose Trail

Another view north during the 1994 charity walk

on the right to Sai Wan Beach. You should be at a concrete crossroads with the trail marked to the right and Sai Wan Road to the left. Beware if you use this as an escape route: you may have to wait more than half an hour at the pagoda-like structure for the registered vehicles that run to Tai Mung Tsai, where the Outward Bound School is located. The path is concreted to Sai Wan Village where you emerge by a cafe and walk through the village. Bear left by two more cafes following the main street - you can cut across the beach in front of you if you want. At the far side of the beach go over a small footbridge to pick up the trail to Ham Tin Beach.

Sai Wan Beach to Chek Keng

Just after Sai Wan Beach, you'll see a sign on your right marking the sunrise in relation to various seasonal solstices. If you get up early enough you will be able to figure out the season from the direction of the sunrise! Also, along the way on the right you can see a village tomb with the characteristic curving roof line above a small doorway, and a designated campsite with

The MacLehose Trail

firepits for cooking. You skirt a beautiful part of the coast with the two rocky outcrops of Tai Chau and Tsim Chau. You come straight onto the beach and are guided through marshy pastures, which often flood after heavy rain. After going around the back of this small, flat bay area, the rough path comes abruptly to a concrete T junction with no signs. Right takes you to the sleepy village of Ham Tin on the northern shore of the beach, with the excellent beachside Hoi Fung store selling iced drinks for $10 and meals from $15.

The MacLehose Trail follows the left fork after crossing a concrete dam over a small stream, which takes you straight to the village of Tai Long. The main businesses appear to be the cafes at the far end of the street. Make sure you go left by the First Stop Cafe which sells meals and soft drinks. <u>DO NOT</u> fork right at the end of the village. This path leads to Sharp Peak and the eastern part of the peninsula. The trail is not marked but Chek Keng is scribbled on a wall and on the path as you exit. See my 'cautionary tale' below about the importance of always being sure where you are going. The path is well-paved as you pass

Descent near Sai Wan

The MacLehose Trail

Tree trimming in Sai Wan village

over Tai Long Au, a saddle between two hills. There's an easy downhill section and you can see the east arm of Long Harbour as you come down. Look for the small ferry which still serves the ramshackle village. Like Tai Long, Chek Keng is semi-deserted, with most of the buildings in a decayed, locked and shuttered state. It is quite beautifully eerie on a sunny evening when the low light reflects off the water and the shadows lengthen around you.

Chek Keng to Pak Tam Au

Just before entering Chek Keng you may take the first path right to the pier which also goes to the youth hostel. If you are not staying the night or taking the ferry to the Chinese University, continue on this path through the first part of the village. At the first split stick with the lower concrete path which leads through a few fields and jinks left uphill shortly after you've passed over a small footbridge. The concrete path goes all the way to Pak Tam Au. It has street lights for part of the way. Shortly, you'll come across trail markers. The last stage is relatively easy with a climb to just over 100 metres. As you near the end of the trail look out for the west arm of Long Harbour with the tiny Wong Shek pier sticking out at its tip. The road climbs around the corner - Ngau Yee Shek Shan, the start of the next part of the trail, will be in front of you. Go left as you exit onto the road to get to the bus stop for Sai Kung or pick up section three on the opposite side of the road. The last downhill walk home is an easy if unspectacular finish to a full and varied day's walk.

2. NATURAL FEATURES AND HISTORY

The most outstanding features of this part of the route are the relatively clean beaches of Sai Wan and Ham Tin. People tell me that ten or fifteen years ago these beaches were virtually unused by the urban population and were not littered with the weekenders' rubbish as they are today. Although the beaches are cleaned by squads of litter pickers, this is no excuse for littering. Use the litter bins provided or take your litter away with you. It is unnerving to visit Long Ke and find swathes of pristine sand at the far end of the beach yet see one of the few bathers sitting next to

Spectacular Ham Tin Wan with the Nam She Tsim (Sharp Peak) range

an overflowing litterbin of festering garbage (possibly feeling homesick for the city). Hong Kong's natural beauty can only survive if the public is strenuous in its efforts to keep it clean—not only for our own enjoyment, but for that of future generations.

The waters here are still very clean and relaxing to swim in - the Pearl River washes most of its rubbish down the western shores of Hong Kong leaving the less settled eastern parts much cleaner. The main threat seems to come not from walkers but from larger numbers of people who come in pleasure boats and anchor off the bays, then go swimming at the beaches. Still, campsite areas around the beaches are often left inexcusably messy, and on a Monday you will see enormous piles of plastic garbage bags filled with the weekend's trash. However, come here during the week and you'd think these beaches were the best kept secret in Hong Kong.

Living History: The Villages of Eastern Saikung

Sadly, the older villages of Tai Long and Chek Keng almost resemble

David Bottomley near Ham Tin

ghost villages, especially if you come midweek when the stores in Tai Long aren't open for day trippers. These villages were originally the home of Hakka peasants who arrived in the area from further north in the 17th century. Not so long ago, the principle export of such villages was rice, but today with the boom in Hong Kong's economy, most of the young have left to pursue the get-rich dream of the city, or have gone abroad in search of the magic dollar. The once dominant village social unit of the extended clan has given way to the more modern nuclear families. Many of the villagers now depend on money sent from relatives working in Hong Kong or other cities or from the dollars of tourists and walkers. In fact I saw more cows than villagers; most of the beasts appeared to be walking the trail in the opposite direction.

The layout of the typical village reflects traditional Chinese rural values based on the geomantic principles of fung shui (literally, 'wind water'), which are supposed to keep away evil spirits and encourage prosperity for the village by locating it favorably in relation to the vital elements. Thus many villages will

A stroll down Tai Wan on an autumn day

High tide near Mong Yue Kok

have protective fung shui woods next to them and will nestle at the bottom of a hill. The houses may be close together in narrow streets to give the community strength and solidarity.

A Cautionary Tale:

Always, Always take a Compass and Map Along

I hope that the following example of my trust in others will impress on people the importance of never going into the hills without a compass and map. The first time I hiked this trail, I went to Sai Kung with the intention of going up Ma On Shan and hiking Section Four, which was the only section I had a map for. The road turned out to be blocked by a landslide so I decided to go to Section Two without a map, my friends having told me it was an easy section and well marked. This was true for the most part, but I was unsure about the direction at the back of Ham Tin village, so I joined another group of hikers. We went through Tai Long and when a thunderstorm broke they insisted we press on because they 'knew where they were going.' We had gone down the path to Sharp Peak (see Directions Section). We ended up wading a swollen stream before the footpath petered out. They only had a small scale map but with the use of my compass it was obvious we were heading away from Chek Keng towards the South China Sea! We retraced our steps to Tai Long and found the less obvious but correct route out.

The motto is always take a compass and map and practice using it. In the end we just got very wet but even this could have been avoided by doing the sensible thing and sheltering whilst the swollen rivers reverted to the trickles they were before the thunderstorm. You should always be sure where you are. Never guess and never trust people with a 'sense of direction' - it could land you in trouble. Even a small twist or turn can completely disorientate you when there are no landmarks around.

3 TRANSPORT AND OTHER DETAILS.
Getting There

There is no public transport directly to Long Ke. See Section

Regular visitors to Sharp Peak meet again

The MacLehose Trail

Villagers on a pier in Long Harbour

One for details of access from Sai Kung. Also see my suggestions for joining Section One with Section Two as far as Chui Tung Au.

Getting Back

To return take bus #94 back to Sai Kung. There is also a #1 minibus on weekends. See Section One for timings.

If you are too tired to hike the last section of the walk to Pak Tam Au, you could catch the 5.00 pm ferry from Chek Keng down the last part of Long Harbour to the Chinese University which is served by the Kowloon-Canton Railroad (KCR). There is also a ferry at around 10.30 in the morning. The ferry probably won't save you much time, but it's an interesting alternative if you want to see the beautiful university at Ma Liu Shui near Shatin. This ferry's principle job is to connect the major urban area of Shatin to Grass Island. It also serves various small villages.

The MacLehose Trail

Accommodation

There's an official campsite on the route just after Sai Wan Beach. A Youth Hostel at Chek Keng known as Bradbury Hall (2328-2458) charges $22 per person. Check-in times are 7-10 am. and 4-11 pm. You aren't allowed to stay in the hostel between 10 a.m. and 4 p.m. There are cooking facilities but no food. Camping is allowed for $10 per person. You must be a member to stay at Youth Hostels in Hong Kong. For details phone the Hong Kong Youth Hostels Association (2788-1638) located at Room 225-6, Block 19, Shep Kip Mei Estate, Kowloon. They will provide full details.

* * * *

Bradbury Hall at Long Harbour (Tai Tan Hoi Hap)

The MacLehose Trail

Section 3
Pak Tam Au to Kei Ling Ha
Difficulty: Grade 3. Time Estimate: 4-5 hours; 10.2 km

Like Section Four that follows it, this is serious hiking but the views are stunning and well worth the effort. Both Sections Three and Four have pros and cons when compared to each other. Section Three is easily reached by bus at both ends, which is not the case with Section Four. The latter, however, includes the drama of Ma On Shan. Both are only for initiated hikers who can cope fairly easily with grade two sections.

This is a day's trip so bring food and water. The main features are the ascent and descent of quite steep volcanic mountains, each climb offering a new vista of the Sai Kung area or of Long Harbour or Three Fathoms Cove to the north. It's wise to pace yourself as there are several climbs of similar difficulty, the last up Kai Kung Shan being perhaps the most difficult. See the profile to get a good idea of the nature of this section.

Sharp Peak and Long Harbour as seen from the Stone Trail

Near Three Fathoms Cove and Ma On Shan at sunrise

The village of Cheung Sheung and adjacent campsite is a good breaking point if you plan to do the trail in a couple of days. There's a small shop at Cheung Sheung where you can stock up on drinks and get a bean curd meal.

The rewards are worth the effort, especially if you go mid-week when you may not see another soul, only the huge expanse of mountains or sea in all directions.

1. ROUTE DETAILS.

From Pak Am Tau to Cheung Sheung Village: Ngau Yee Shek Shan and Ngam Tau Shan

If continuing from Section Two of the route, turn left on the road and walk 30 metres to pick up the trail on the opposite side. You'll find a large wooden sign and information board. If doing the route separately, continue on bus #94 past Pak Tam Chung terminus until you see the signpost for the trail on the left. You can also ask the driver for Pak Tam Au. This is the tiny village

The MacLehose Trail

Stone Trail near Pak Tam Au

on the right opposite the start of Section Three.

The trail starts with a steep climb up a stepped footpath. There are two initial steep sections which are in fact the ascent of Ngau Yee Shek Shan and Ngam Tau Shan. The route then diverts to the left of the 451m Ngam Tau Shan. After about 1km a smaller path leads to its summit, which isn't on the trail. As you come over Ngau Yee Shek to the small plateau between the hills you can see the radio masts in the distance. There are superb views all around you.

Around the southern side of Ngam Tau Shan a great view of a valley and distant hills opens up before you to the west. As you descend on the other side towards Cheung Sheung, the valley leads away to the Sai Kung Bay area to your left. The path follows the south side of Ngam Tau Shan to the forest just before the village of Cheung Sheung. The trail is clearly marked at a split just as you enter the forest. The path then weaves over tree routes washed bare by summer rains. You emerge at a campsite behind which is the village (little more than a few corrugated metal dwellings). To pick up the trail follow the marker as you enter the campsite but beware - do not take the path also signposted for the toilets as this peters out behind the campsite (the trail sign post is unclear).

Cheung Sheung is a nice place to camp if it's kept clean by those who use it.

From Cheung Sheung to Kai Kung Shan: Wa Mei Shan and Lui Ta Shek

At the back of Cheung Sheung the trail descends into a lush forest and crosses a small stream where, in the rainy season, you may have to get your feet wet. You emerge and climb the eastern side of Wa Mei Shan. The path drops down steeply as you bend west round the southern side of Wa Mei Shan and you can see the path fork at the bottom of the path. There are no signposts but take either path as they rejoin each other. Ahead you can see the hill of Lui Ta Shek marked by two large boulders. Descend to the fork in the trail, go through a brief patch of forest, and climb

A fish farm in Long Harbour

The MacLehose Trail

over a mini pass between Lui Ta Shek on your left and another unnamed hill on your right.

The trail then descends steeply in places and the impressive peak of Kai Kung Shan can be seen rising sharply in front of you with a rocky face marked by steep waterfalls in the rainy season – this is the last real climb. During much of this middle section of the trail, you'll see Three Fathoms Cove and the village of Yung Shue O to your right. At the foot of Kai Kung Shan you'll come to a small ridge with a sign giving safety hints to hikers. A footpath off to the left leads to Shek Hang Village – you may be able to hear the dogs in the distance! This is a good escape route in bad weather: it takes you through the village to a small road leading south to join the main coastal road. As you emerge onto the road catch bus #94 going back to Sai Kung. The only other village you go through on the escape route is Tai Po Tsai so follow signs for this when on the minor road. It's about 5km downhill from the trail to the road.

Gurkhas taking a rest between Sections 3 and 4

Over Kai Kung Shan to the Kei Ling Ha Road

The ascent lasts only about 1km but is quite steep in places and can be very slippery when wet. At the bottom on your left is a small wooded valley. You may be able to hear the stream running through it. The trail up comes up to two T junctions in the path, go left at both. The last junction takes you to the summit of Kai Kung Shan with a nearly 360 degree panorama.

The trail can be clearly seen from the summit descending over two smaller hills and around the southern side of a third. After the hills, the trail goes down into scrub forest for what seems like a long last kilometre and a half, before exiting on the road where bus #99 or #299 goes south (to your left) to Sai Kung.

2. NATURAL FEATURES AND HISTORY

The most amazing parts of this section are the many views ranging over much of the eastern New Territories and north to China. The views from Ngam Tau Shan and especially from Kai Kung Shan make it clear that much of Hong Kong and especially the Sai Kung peninsula are composed of what were once deep valleys that have been filled in by the sea or by eroded earth slipping down the steep volcanic slopes. In fact, Tolo Harbour was once a deep land valley.. It is easy to see why the area attracted so much pirate activity in previous centuries, at one point prompting the Chinese Emperor to order the evacuation of a strip of land around this coastal area to deprive the pirates of their mainland trading bases. The high-sided inlets would have made ideal shelters to hide out in.

The first peak is Ngau Yee Shek Shan, which means ' Cow's Ear Hill', perhaps reflecting the ancient Chinese tradition of giving a plate of cow ears to a chosen leader. From Ngam Tau Shan it is possible to see Sharp Peak behind and to the left of Pak Tam Au. Note the small cultivated terraces behind Pak Tam Au. To the north you can see Long Harbour and the ferry going to Grass

The MacLehose Trail

Island, used by Hong Kongers at weekends as a quiet refuge to indulge in one of their favourite pastimes, dining on seafood. To the south is much of the Sai Kung Bay area.

The valley after Wa Ma Shan is typical of the deep green scenery that dominates much of the central Sai Kung peninsula. In the distance you may be able to see the strange space-age construction that is the Lady MacLehose Holiday Village. Looking in the other direction towards Kai Kung Shan, you can see the fish farms by the village of Yung Shue O come into view. These floating fish cages are an alternative to traditional fishing methods, which have become increasingly inefficient as the bays have become fished out. Here is one of 28 designated fish culture zones in Hong Kong, a kind of marine equivalent to battery hens.

The views from the triangulation point on top of Kai Kung Shan are best of all. You can see almost the whole length of Tolo Harbour with Plover Cove Reservoir in the background, and the taller Pat Sin range of mountains behind this. In front of you on the trail lies the distinctive shape of Ma On Shan. Behind you can see much of the eastern peninsula and High Island Reservoir.

Living History on the Descent to Kei Ling Ha.
Ancestral Shrines

As you approach the main road through the wood on the last part of the trail you will see two small concrete shrines containing a number of jars. These are the graves of villagers' ancestors, which are the centerpiece of the important ancient Chinese tradition of ancestry worship.

According to Chinese tradition the dead must be cared for and appeased. Although part of their soul will go to the underworld, part will perhaps go to the ancestral hall and another part will remain here on earth. It is a Chinese belief that the dead must be ritually 'fed and honoured' or they will return to be mischievous after death. At the Ching Ming Festival, the family

The MacLehose Trail

Trailwalker Station at Sai Sha Road

visits the graves of their ancestors, making offerings and celebrating with a picnic feast.

Traditionally only male offspring are allowed to worship ancestors, which is a large part of why males are considered so valuable in rural Chinese society.

TRANSPORT AND OTHER DETAILS.

Getting There

To get to the start of the trail take bus #94 from Sai Kung terminus - see transport details for Section One and also the route details for this section above.

Getting Away

The trail descends onto a picnic area. Catch a bus left (south) back to Sai Kung - walk north on the road round the bend to get to a stop. Of course you can also get back to town via Shatin then board the KCR.

The MacLehose Trail

#99 - KMB - From Lai Chung.
Last bus: Weekdays - 7.37 p.m.
Sundays and public holidays - 7.15 p.m.
Every hour.
#299 - KMB - From Shatin Central to Sai Kung.
Last bus: 11.00 p.m.
Every 9 to 20 minutes.

Campsites

The only campsite on this section is at Cheung Sheung about 3.5 km after the start of the section. Camping is free. It's not advisable to drink the stream water here.

* * * *

Kai Kung Shan is next

The MacLehose Trail

Excursion 1 (MacLehose No. 4)
Sai Kung to Kwong Yuen Estate

The walk from Sai Kung to Kwong Yuen Estate near Shatin is about 6 km with a sharp elevation from sea level to 600m. Allow 4 hours for the walk and two hours for travel in order to enjoy it. Degree of difficulty: 4 in fair weather and 5 if it has rained (generally not advisable). Only attempt this walk in company and with superior footwear and gloves. Do not try it if you have fear of heights!

The South China Sea can be reached over water from most towns and villages in Hong Kong. Tai Po and Shatin, for example, are directly connected with the sea through Tolo Harbour, and Sai Kung through Rocky Bay. Shatin and Sai Kung are separated by the mountain range that falls under the Ma On Shan Country Park. It used to be difficult to get from this one village to the next though they are so close to each other by air.

But since both towns grew rapidly in the eighties, a decision

Walking club sets out from Sai Kung

The MacLehose Trail

was made to build in rapid succession the Hang On, Yiu On and Ma On Shan Estates near the the promontory of Wu Kwai Sha Tsui (now the infamous Whitehead detention centre for Vietnamese boat people) overlooking Tolo Harbour. Improved infrastructure was a matter of time. There is now an excellent road called Sai Sha Road that allows you to travel between Shatin and Sai Kung within 15 minutes.

In Magic Walks 13, 34 and 44, we covered three alternative routes crossing Ma On Shan Country Park between these two towns. Today we are adding a very exciting alternative trail. It follows the MacLehose Trail for about 1.5 km and offers an excellent escape route in two directions. To get to the starting point, take the public light bus (PLB) No.1, also called minibus No. 1, to Sai Kung from Choi Hung Estate. They leave every few minutes at any time of the day right in front of the MTR northern exit on Clearwater Bay Road. Before you board, you could buy fruits and soft drinks at the main covered market adjacent to the MTR exit.

There is no need to stay on

Direction Ngong Ping

The MacLehose Trail

Near Pyramid Hill

this PLB all the way to the end. Ask the bus driver to stop on Hiram's Highway the moment that your minibus enters Sai Kung itself, i.e. when the first row of houses and shops appear on the left. Get off and walk back to the road that is then on your right and that leads to Po Lo Che (see photo on page 45). Walk uphill and stay on this road until you get to a crossroads where four streets meet.

Take the second one left that leads gradually uphill (called Pak Kong Au Road). There is a noodles and soft drink store on the right. It is your last chance to stock up; this is no luxury on a hot day as there is nothing you can buy until you reach Shatin. This road leads past the Sai Kung H/L Pump House (left) and Mou Ping New Village (on the right). You will see many Spanish villas, the favourite New Territories model. The street then curves left when you come to Tai Shui Tseng hamlet right ahead. The other small village on the left is called Pak Kong Au.

On this corner (i.e. immediately on the right) in front of DD222 Wong Shuk Shan, there is a little trail indicated by the blue Chinese characters (行山) which stand for 'Haahng Shaan' or 'Walk

The MacLehose Trail

Sai Kung and Rocky Bay (background).

Mountain'. This path would take you to Ngong Ping on the MacLehose Trail if you went straight uphill. Follow it for about 200m, when you will see the (Tai Shui Tseng) water storage tank on the right. Turn left over here (and thus not uphill) and start the gradually rising contour walk.

The path is good and takes you to the camping and barbecue site where the MacLehose Trail crosses the trail to Mau Ping and Mui Tsz Lam (Magic Walk 34). The path from Pak Kong mentioned in that walk joins your trail when you near the crest. As soon as you reach the crossroads, the camping plateau is on your left. You may want a breather here as you have just climbed 300m from sea level. Follow the sign that says 'Gilwell Camp'. We shall not go that far today, but are taking the MacLehose Trail until it comes to Buffalo Pass. It is a gradual climb with a 10% gradient most of the way to 500 m above sea level, although the path dips twice at the start. The two distinctive Buffalo Hills rise in front of you.

Exactly opposite the trail that leads down to Sam Fai Tan (and Pak Wai and Pak Sha Wan) you have to start your assault on Buffalo Hill (Shui Ngau Shan). It is a faint path that leads steeply

The MacLehose Trail

uphill at a 25% angle until you reach the highest point (marker with 'Trigonometrical station'). You must turn a full 120% to the right at this stage to begin the precarious journey along the ridge to the next mountain range.

I have made this climb in cloudy weather three times when there was a good deal of wind or lots of clouds with hardly any visibility. Such weather tends to create a magical atmosphere. You may, however, prefer to make this climb in October or November when you will seldom be handicapped in this manner. But, as already said, my experience shows that it is perfectly possible to do it under adverse conditions. However, never do it alone since the next two kilometres will be very treacherous and a false step could find you sliding a hundred metres or so down a slope. Especially rainy weather would make your step suspect unless you carefully watch where you put your feet at all times, one step at a time.

The path to take is the one in an exact northerly direction crossing to Shek Nga Shan. On a clear day, it gives stunning

A good slug of water before tackling Buffalo Hill

The MacLehose Trail

views in all directions. This is not for the faint-hearted as the path is quite narrow at times on both sides and the drop quite steep; a bit like the trail from Ma On Shan to the Hunchbacks (Magic Walk No. 44). Near Shek Nga Shan you will reach a ridge which tends to be a good spot to have an orange stop or a spot of lunch. There is another path that continues in the same direction, but I do not recommend it. Turn instead to the left (north-west and downhill). The descent is then rather steep but not too difficult to manage in dry weather.

Once you have come down from the 600 m level to 400 m above Shatin, the drop of the trail becomes more gradual. The path starts pointing west-south-west in the direction of Shatin. Nui Po Shan (Turret Hill) appears on the right. The last stretch towards Kwong Yuen Estate is very steep again but there is now plenty of vegetation which allows you to hold on to it. You should come down near a couple of graves which connect to the main trail between Wong Nai Tau and Mui Tsz Lam (Magic Walk 34) which is concreted.

The map on this path erected by the Shatin District Board indicates that you have just completed part of their 'white route'. Turn left here in the direction of Shatin, cross the small bridge and turn right. This path will lead you steadily downhill, another 500m to the hamlets of Tai Che, Fa Sam Hang and Wong Nai Tau. A lot of paths have been reconstructed here in the last year but common sense will take you to the bus stop. You can take PLB 65K to Shatin Town Hall and the KCR station from where the urban area is within easy reach.

If you are thirsty, then soft drinks and fruits can be bought at the market in Kwong Yuen Estate, a mere three-minute walk down the road from Wong Nai Tau where other public transport, like buses, could take you directly to Kowloon.

* * * *

The MacLehose Trail

Section 4
Kei Ling Ha to Tate's Cairn
Difficulty: Grade 3. Time Estimate: 5-6 hours; 12.7 km

This is one of the hardest walks on the MacLehose Trail. There are several steep climbs, but the scenery is dramatic, different and highly recommended. You start off at the edge of Sai Kung east; access is from the town of Sai Kung. Heading southwest, you pass through the mountain ranges of Ma On Shan Country Park to the start of Lion Rock Country Park.

This section starts with a gentle rise through woodland. The approach to Ma On Shan becomes increasingly spectacular as the trail steepens and you can see the craggy features of the mountain's eastern face. The climb to the ridge of Ma On Shan is not for the faint-hearted and it's best to have some hiking experience and to be in good shape. You will find yourself taking big steps going up as you leave the woodland behind. This is one of the hardest but most rewarding climbs on the whole trail.

Overlooking Sai Kung and Rocky Harbour

The MacLehose Trail

Three Fathoms Cove and Tolo Harbour as seen from Ma On Shan

In between the rugged peaks of Ma On Shan and the Buffalo Hills, you can enjoy the serenity of the Ngong Ping Plateau. On a weekday I saw only one other person for the whole of the walk. After the climb out of the plateau there's another steep grade before hitting the final, easier part of the trail to Gilwell Campsite and the road. Add an hour on to the time estimate to allow for the exit at the end of the trail (see Transport). You will have to walk or hitch down Fei Ngo Shan Road to Choi Hung MTR at the finish, unless continuing on to Section Five.

This is easily a full day's trip. If you want to amble along this section and take in the sights, you can break at the Ngong Ping Plateau campsite overnight, and complete the trip the next day.

1. ROUTE DETAILS

From Kei Ling Ha to Ngong Ping Plateau

Take bus #99 or #299 from Sai Kung to Kei Ling Ha. About

five minutes after the bus has turned left at a roundabout up Ma On Shan Road, you'll see a picnic area on the right. Get off the next stop and walk back past a tree walk on your right. The start of Section Four is a footpath to the side of the road opposite the picnic site (the exit point of Section Three). Better still would be to take a taxi. A taxi driver can take you straight to the correct spot, which could be missed by bus.

Follow this footpath until you join a concrete road. After about ten minutes turn left. Shortly, you will join Chuk Yeung Road by turning right . You're going around the south side of a small hill and you can see Sai Kung to your left. Ma On Shan comes into view around the next corner. The valley below is scarred with the effects of mining. At the next crossroads take the signpost left and find yourself on a broad mud path. Look out for the isolated village of Wong Chuk Yeung on the right. Go right by the water pipes then split off left and start to climb at some small stone steps by a little stream.

The climb gets steeper here, leveling out after twenty min-

Whitehead Detention Centre and Plover Cove as seen from Tiu Shau Ngam

The MacLehose Trail

Shatin and valley

utes and you'll see Ma On Shan again. The path now threads through the wooded mounded hills, ultimately heading just to the left of Ma On Shan. There's a plateau before you climb what is the steepest part of the section. Be careful on the ascent and stick to the path. There are steep drops on either side of the path. You can see villages dotting the side of Three Fathoms Cove and the fish farms floating in the middle of the inlet.

Coming to the gentle pass at the top of the climb, Ma On Shan rises majestically on your right. If you want a spectacular diversion you can go up Ma On Shan on this right-hand path, but the trail itself leads off left. It cuts into the side of a smaller hill before dropping down to the bottom of Pyramid Hill. On the level section you see the steep profile of a peninsula of Ma On Shan which masks a disused quarry. On the knoll there is a path to Pyramid Hill - bear right. After following the valley floor see signposts for Hang On Estate (a good escape route in bad weather), Kei Ling Ha (the path you've come on), and Gilwell Campsite and the MacLehose Trail to the left.

The MacLehose Trail

Ngong Ping to Buffalo Pass

The drama of the climb gives way to serene grassland and the Ngong Ping Campsite is to your right. There is a posted map of the area after the campsite. Left is Hiram's Highway (2.6 km) and Pak Kong Au Village (1.3km). Hiram's Highway is the coastal road that goes past Marina Cove; if you want to head off early, take this path and catch bus #92 to Choi Hung.

Straight ahead on the trail, a string of three mountains is your next target. The higher peaks on the right are the Buffalo Hills - you will go between these and the smaller Calf's Head on the left over Buffalo Pass. Going towards the hills, the yachting bay of Hebe Haven is on your left and Razor Hill is behind it in the distance. After going round the side of a hill with this vista on your left, drop down to a junction in some woods. The villages of Mau Ping (Lo Uk and San Uk) are signposted right. This path eventually joins a road near Shatin. After going through a picnic site with Mui Tsz Lam signposted right the climb begins in earnest. At this junction go straight on for Gilwell Campsite.

Sai Kung and South China Sea

The MacLehose Trail

Going up the plateau before Calf's Head, the rough peaks of West Buffalo Hill and Buffalo Hill resemble Siamese twins – identical peaks strangely fused in the middle. Close to Calf's Head the pass brings you to the head of a valley, which opens before you as you come over the rise.

Buffalo Pass to Section 5

On top of Buffalo Pass, there's a path to the right over the two Buffalo peaks towards Shatin, about 5km. Tate's Cairn is roughly the same distance. You can now aim for Tate's Cairn radio masts in front of you. The trail is visible going round the back of Buffalo Hill above a valley. The back of the trail is now broken - gently drop down for about one kilometre then through a small wood at the head of a valley with Marina's Cove at the end. Coming out of the wood you are on the side of Heather Hill (which does have heather on it).

It's not clear where the path is heading at this point but it leads to a short, steep climb around the back of the aptly named 'One More Rise'. At the end of this rise is a nice picnic spot in a wooded glade. Out of the glade is Gilwell

Ma On Shan and ridge to the Hunchbacks

Campsite. The path joins a small concrete road. Left takes you to Fei Ngo Shan Road T junction. Go left to Clear Water Bay Road, then right to Choi Hung MTR. You should be able to hitchhike once you hit Fei Ngo Shan Road . If you are going on to Section Five, make a right when you come onto the small concrete road after Gilwell Campsite signs.

View east from near Ngong Ping

2. NATURAL FEATURES AND HISTORY

Ma On Shan, which means 'horse's saddle mountain' in Cantonese, is one of the most unusually shaped and precipitous hills in all of Hong Kong . It links with other hills made of the same hard volcanic rock as Pyramid Hill and the Buffalo Hills. Viewed on your approach from the southeast it's not apparent the extent to which man's activity has changed the landscape of Ma On Shan. On the opposite side a large iron mine has dramatically altered the aspect of the hill from the west. Hakka peasants cleared many of the slopes here in centuries past to cultivate tea and indigo. Although these local peasant cottage industries have all but

The MacLehose Trail

disappeared, they have left an indelible mark on the appearance of the land around Ma On Shan.

Although the iron mine was only productive for a few decades it employed several hundred people, many of whom settled in the area when the mine closed and whose descendants now inhabit nearby villages.

You can see the extent to which the eastern Sai Kung seaboard has become the playground of the wealthy when you look out over Hebe Haven Bay and Marina Cove, packed with expensive pleasure boats and surrounded by luxury apartments.

3. TRANSPORT AND OTHER DETAILS.

Getting There

Bus #92 from Choi Hung MTR to Sai Kung - see Section One for details.

From Sai Kung to Kei Ling Ha: Bus #99 or #299 - for details see Section Three.

Getting Away

See above details and map. There is no public transport at the end of Section Four. When descending from Gilwell Campsite go left on the small concrete road. See the directions above.

Accommodation

There are no Youth Hostels on this section, only the following campsites:

On the right after joining the first concrete road. About 15 minutes walk from the start of the section.

Ngong Ping Plateau Campsite - after about 5.5km.

Gilwell Campsite - at the end of the section. This must be

booked through the Kowloon Scouts Association, Regional Headquarters, Unit 1-7 Ground Floor, Tung Mun House, Tai Hang Estate. Telephone: 27882811

* * * *

"Orange stop" near Gilwell Campsite

The MacLehose Trail

Section 5
Tate's Cairn to Tai Po Road
Difficulty: Grade 2. Time Estimate: 3-4 hours; 10.6 km

This section is most convenient for city dwellers who want quick access to the countryside but who are still looking for a challenge. It doesn't require the time or preparation necessary to go to the comparative wilds of Sai Kung. Access at both ends of the route from the urban area of the Kowloon peninsula is relatively easy once you know the points of departure and arrival, although you should add a bit to the walking time estimate as you'll have to take a taxi, then walk to the start of the route. An hour should be plenty.

This section is ideal when your time is restricted to one valuable free day a week, when you really want to get away. It's in-

On Stokers Hill looking north

The MacLehose Trail

credible how the place you might perceive as noisy, polluted and overcrowded from street level can become quite enthralling from a height. You might even see buildings and features you walked straight past without ever noticing.

The walk takes you above Kowloon and Shatin. After Tates's Cairn there's an easy walk mainly on the road to Shatin Pass where you face the only steep climb of about a kilometre. This puts you on the track to Lion Rock. This section is ideal to get a new perspective on the busy metropolis of Hong Kong.

Wong Tai Sin Temple and Lion Rock in the background

One of the main features in this section is ridge-walking. Many of the hills in Hong Kong are linked by a spine which is very convenient for going from peak to peak without having to struggle down into a valley and back up a steep climb, as is the case for the more difficult Section Three. On this walk you will go on or near many of the peaks that form the well-known backdrop to Kowloon (the 'nine dragons' for which Kowloon is named).

The route from Lion Rock to Beacon Hill is quite leisurely as

The MacLehose Trail

Our walking club after a Section 5 hike

long as you watch where you are going. There are a couple of minor climbs approaching Beacon Hill but if you take these slowly they aren't a real problem. There's no extended climb on this section.

The last part of the section drops down and, again, all that's required is a little careful footwork. Some of the steps have a concrete lip which needs negotiation. The descent to Tai Po Road is mainly stepped but steep in places. Bear this in mind if doing the trail in the opposite direction. Eventually you will follow a nature trail through woods, which is the least taxing part of the walk, and an ideal opportunity to experience quiet natural surroundings after the dramatic heights looking over the city.

1. **ROUTE DETAILS**

Tate's Cairn to Shatin Pass

This section starts just before Tate's Cairn in the depression between the mountains of Buffalo Hill and Tate's Cairn.

The MacLehose Trail

From Choi Hung MTR Station take a taxi up Fei Ngo Shan Road. You must get out at the road leading off Fei Ngo Shan Road which goes to Gilwell Campsite. Ask the driver for 'Fei Ngo Shan Lo' and when on this road ask for the Gilwell Campsite. The road you want is on a hairpin and leads due north whilst Fei Ngo Shan Road loops in a southerly direction. Go down this small concrete road for about 0.5km, going left at the first split, then left at the next T junction. Shortly, the road opens into a large clear area where the trail follows a footpath which hairpins off the road to your left. You'll find an emergency telephone here. Mau Tso Ngam village is on the road to the right and straight on is Fu Yung Pit. These two places are very tiny hamlets.

Having joined the footpath a small climb gives way to a twenty-minute hike through woodland before climbing to Tate's Ridge. In the rainy season the sound of streams nearby rushing down the hillside and a myriad of beautifully coloured insects give this jungle section a uniquely serene feel. Suddenly the path takes a sharp left away from the jungle and you tack up a mod-

Lion Rock seen from near Beacon Hill

The MacLehose Trail

erately steep climb to an area to the right of some radio masts. Shatin is in the distance to your right behind Temple Hill (surrounded by villages) and the distinctive Sugar Loaf Peak. There is a scruffy-looking concrete area with a number of dead ends. Pick up a left towards the police post. The trail is signposted from the front of the police post and onto the broad steps that lead down to the Shatin Pass area.

"Trail" walkers (1992) approaching Beacon Hill

The path then meets Fei Ngo Shan Road where you turn right. At the next road junction in front of you, go straight on past the 'no entry' signs. The road joining from the left is Jat's Incline, which would take you to Clear Water Bay Road and Choi Hung MTR. There is no public transport here, but there is a car park which provides easy access if you want to pick up the route at this stage.

As you go down the road, there's a steep hill with a radio mast to your right and a view over Kai Tak Airport to your left. There are small squatter villages below you. The road cuts through a small hill with a triangulation point just to your left. You reach the bottom of this descent at a road junction, Shatin Pass, where you will see a cafe on your right. You can use the road to Shatin

The MacLehose Trail

on the right if you want to end the route early. Shatin is a 4km walk. Continue straight on and at the next hairpin you should see a large wooden gate leading you up the hill towards Lion Rock, away from the road which doubles back to Tsz Wan Shan Housing Estate.

Shatin Pass to Beacon Hill

This is one of the climbs where you'll need to slow down a little, especially in summer, but it's largely steps so there's no real physical difficulty. Looking back you can see a large quarry behind Kowloon Peak. Leveling out, the path takes you behind Lion Rock Hill and you can now see Shatin to the right. On a clear day look for the distinctive Needle Hill and Tai Mo Shan to the northwest. There's a path about 1.2km after Shatin Pass for Tsz Wan Shan Housing Estate (marked 1.3km) from where you can get a cab or walk to Choi Hung MTR. Here you pass behind Lion Rock without ever getting a clear view of it.

Shortly, there's another path to Lion Rock that you can use as

The ridge between Beacon Hill and Lion Rock

The MacLehose Trail

Trailwalker Station on Beacon Hill

an alternative route if you want to look at the rock itself. You could then pick up the trail by turning west. (Check the map). Amah Rock comes into view on your right. Follow a number of electricity pylons before turning south across Lion Rock Hill through a wooded area. The wood lasts for about 1km. It includes a small but steep muddy drop where the steps are washed away and you need to be careful.

Eventually you exit past a small shelter, where you'll find a large junction of paths. You can cut short your journey by taking the path signposted 'Catchwater 0.7km', and pick up the Hung Mui Kuk Nature Trail, finishing on Lion Rock Tunnel Road. If you do that, you will exit at a T junction, then go right and follow the water catchment until you see the sign down to the main road (near Amah Rock). From here you can get a bus back to Kowloon. Notice the strange linear layout of Shatin on your descent. There's also a signposted, longer descent in the same direction to the water catchment via Amah Rock. Use the signpost for Wang Tau Hom Housing Estate, in the exact opposite direction, to cut back to the Kowloon peninsula if

The MacLehose Trail

you fancy retiring early; but you'll miss one of the best parts of the trail towards Beacon Hill if you do. In Wang Tau Hom you can get a cab or walk back to Lok Fu MTR.

The MacLehose Trail continues along the ridge (at this junction); in a short while you can look back at Lion Rock emerging grandly from the top of the hill. To the north you can make out its less dramatic neighbour Amah Rock, the view slightly obscured by a pylon. This is good place to observe all the Kowloon landmarks. The path is clear as it leads you to Beacon Hill with the golf ball-like structures on top.

The path climbs the southern side of Beacon Hill.

Beacon Hill to Section 6

Pass in front of the first radar station and cross straight over the feeder road that services the beacons. You should see another dome on your left and then hit the triangulation point marking

Trailwalkers signing in before the descent to Tai Po Road

The MacLehose Trail

Near Tai Po Road on Eagle's Nest nature trail

the top of Beacon Hill. The Kowloon Reservoir is in front of you. On the descent, cross over the feeder road two more times. The heavy industrial area of west Kowloon is on your left on the first part of the descent. Further down there's a split at a shelter. A nature trail is signposted left and the MacLehose Trail to the right. A further split is signposted left. You have now joined Eagle's Nest Nature Trail. You should encounter a signposted vantage point of Tai Mo Shan and Needle and Grassy Hills. This is a good place to get your bearings if you're heading for these later sections. The route twists and turns but the path is always wide and easy to follow. The exit comes onto a small concrete road. Go right towards the main road. There's an information board to help you as you come to the road.

If you're continuing on to Section Six, go right along the main road then make an immediate left towards Kowloon Reservoir up Golden Hill Road. If you decide it's time to head home there's a bus stop a short way down the road to the left where you can pick up bus #72 to Tai Kok Tsui Ferry Pier or one of the many minibuses that end up in Sham Shui Po and Mongkok.

The MacLehose Trail

2. NATURAL FEATURES AND HISTORY

At various points on the ridge you can stop and watch the planes as the aircraft seem to float in front of you before smoothly touching down. You could study the numerous details of the cityscape for hours. All the famous landmarks on Hong Kong Island and Kowloon are visible. Look for the cemetery (a pyramidal structure near the airport) and the container terminal with crane arms sticking up like cocktail sticks. Hong Kong appears as a truly futuristic metropolis with the huge tankers squatting in the harbour and helicopters buzzing overhead. A smaller scale map with major landmarks can help those less familiar with the area identify exactly what they are looking at. On a clear day you can also see the Lantau mountains and even Castle Peak in the western distance.

Living History — Chinese Myths of Amah and Lion Rocks

These may just be strangely shaped rocks to overseas visitors but to the Chinese locals, Mong Fu Sek and Sz Tsz Shan (their respective Cantonese names) are the

Trail walkers near Kowloon Reservoir

69

source of time-honoured fables that have been passed down from generation to generation.

Mong Fu Shek is supposed to have been the lookout point of a fisherman's wife who, with her baby, waited in vain for the return of her missing husband. The gods took pity on her and transported her to heaven leaving this reminder in her place. In another account a Soong dynasty bodyguard fled the area, leaving his wife and child wandering the hills looking for him. Eventually they died and turned to stone. From most vantage points, the rock clearly resembles a woman carrying her baby on her back in the Chinese fashion.

Lion Rock is in fact supposed to resemble a number of things, not only a lion but also the head of a tiger or an otter, take your pick! The large number of rocks that have become sites for local pilgrimages in Hong Kong is not mere idiosyncrasy. It is a deeply held belief in Chinese culture that visits to such sites, especially on significantly portentous dates, can influence your future.

On Beacon Hill, you are standing only a few hundred feet above the KCR. You can see Needle Hill to the north and Shing Mun Reservoir – the finish of Stage 6 and start of Stage 7. This is another great viewpoint and a good spot to stop for a picnic lunch. When I was here on a fine summer's day, most of Lantau Island was clearly visible except for Lantau Peak, which had its head stuck in the clouds. There was also a view of the harbour reclamation project in the west of Kowloon. It's definitely worth picking a clear day for this section.

The latter part of Section 5 joins the nature trail marked by luxuriant foliage well documented by information boards. It's also a good place to observe exciting wildlife.

Natural History of Eagle's Nest Hill (Tsim Shan)

This hill is actually misnamed in English. It is home not to the eagle but to the black-eared kite which breeds here. You may catch a glimpse of this large bird of prey (65cm wingspan) soaring above the hills. It's the most common bird of prey and found throughout much of Hong Kong.

I also noticed a troop of Macaque monkeys sitting in the trees on the lower part of the nature trail, near rubbish bins. They are used to humans and may expect food. If you antagonise them they may bite you, which is not only painful but may infect you with a disease. They are wild animals, not pets. They are quite safe if you treat them as such and respect them. If you are approached aggressively it's best to stay calm and the monkey will most likely back off. There are three types of Macaque, Rhesus, long- tailed and Tibetan. Rhesus macaques are the only ones you might see in groups. The end of Section Five or the start of Section Six are the most likely sighting spots.

3. TRANSPORT AND OTHER DETAILS

Getting There

To access Tate's Cairn go to the Choi Hung MTR and take the Civic Centre exit. This will bring you to the road leading to Sai Kung – Clearwater Bay Road. The quickest way is to take a cab from here as the road leading to Tate's Cairn is not served by public transport. Ask the driver for Fei Ngo Shan Lo. This is the road that goes up the eastern side of Kowloon Peak (Fei Ngo Shan). The driver should keep bearing right on this road. When on Fei Ngo Shan Road, ask for the road to Gilwell Campsite. As you travel up, you'll see great views of Kowloon and Kowloon Peak on your left.

If you want to extend the first part of the journey you could get bus #92 from outside Choi Hung MTR, to the bottom of Fei Ngo Shan Road and walk up it. Do not go onto Jat's Incline which is a similar road that leads up the western side of Kowloon Peak.

For the times of bus #92 see Section One.

Getting Away

After arriving at Tai Po Road, bus #72 will take you back to Tai Kok Tsui (left) or onto Tai Po (right). For the times see the end of the next section.

Accommodation

There are no designated campsites on this section. There is one cafe at Shatin Pass before the climb that goes behind Lion Rock.

* * * *

Squatter village near Wang Tau Hom (at the foot of Lion Rock)

The MacLehose Trail

Excursion 2 (MacLehose Nos. 6 & 7)
Tai Wai to Tsuen Wan

The walk from Tai Wai to Tsuen Wan or Kwai Chung is about 6 km. It has a slight elevation of 200 m, but for some of the path you would need good footwear and a sense of balance in adverse weather conditions. Allow for 2.5 hours to really enjoy it. Degree of difficulty: 3. 4 in bad weather.

This is the perfect walk to contemplate if you have just half a day to spare. Both the starting and finishing points are within easy reach of the public transport system. Take the KCR to Tai Wai (the stop between Kowloon Tong and Shatin).

Right in front of the station, you can buy all you need as

Lower Shing Mun Reservoir in April

The MacLehose Trail

refreshment. The little square outside the station is on the northwest side. After you have stocked up, walk along the railroad in the direction you came from by train (southwest) and cross the main road (Hung Mui Kuk Road). The street you are taking will swing right after 300 m like a crescent moon rising slowly and bringing you to the traffic lights that regulate the unending drone of container trucks along Tai Po Road.

Continue on the same street on the other side. The Shatin District Board has set out a number of trails on the map on that corner: you will be taking most of the 'brown route'. The road continues to rise for a while but then quickly starts descending and is now called Lower Shing Mun Road. Ignore the first road on the right (that leads to Tai Wai New Village) and also the steep road to the left that leads to the mortuary and two sets of fine villas on top of the hill. When you reach the Fushan Crematorium, the road zigzags down and then

Looking west from the trail

The MacLehose Trail

Required dress: very, very casual

turns left in a semi-circle; it starts then leading sharply uphill until it reaches the dam to the Lower Shing Mun Reservoir.

Spring flowers near the dam (Lower Shing Mun)

The MacLehose Trail

Along the ridge

It is possible to reach our destination the (Higher) Shing Mun or Jubilee Reservoir along the north shore, but having tried both, I want to introduce you today to the southern approach, a very enjoyable little trail. Turn left when you are level with the dam, i.e. directly south into the direction of the midday sun and away from the main dam. Walk about 50 m until you notice the distinctive square wooden pole with the S-sign of the Shatin District Board. Your right turn is blocked by a barrier and the sign 'no through road'. This is the path you must take; the road itself leads to nowhere and is only for the benefit of the Water Authority. Your own trail starts with the partially decayed wooden stairs 50 m onwards on the left along the waterpipe.

Since there is no way that you can get lost once you are on it, I am not going to describe the little surprises that you are going to discover along the way. The only thing I shall do is to warn you that it is more difficult than you would imagine by studying the maps. Though the Country Park Authority started to repair the path some time ago, they stopped for some reason and the

The MacLehose Trail

steps have fallen into decay again. If you are not careful in slippery weather, you could easily slide 5-7 m down at certain points. There are a couple of rocks where your ascent and descent is made easier by ropes and chains. It becomes a dangerous operation without these, as you will duly see.

When you near the end of the regular path, you may be astonished to hear traffic zooming past. The reason is that they built a tunnel from Tai Wai to Tsuen Wan a few years ago, and the only open section that allows a bit of light and the very necessary oxygen for the users of this long tunnel is the bridge that emerges from one mountain wall and disappears into the next across the Reservoir.

At this exact point, the path s u d d e n l y swerves left and runs along a small ravine. During the rainy season (from April to September) a lot of water tends to come down Smuggler's Pass and drops down into the Reservoir via the catchwater. Part of the other side is a catchwater and is easily navigated. You will find an ini-

Zooming traffic; Tai Wai - Tsuen Wan

The MacLehose Trail

tially broad set of steps on the left. At this point you could continue until you reach the dam of the Upper Jubilee Reservoir. It can only be climbed if it is totally dry as there are no steps on this side. It is therefore best to finish the trail by using the abovementioned steps. It merges at the top with one of the trails that come down from Smuggler's Ridge and Kowloon Reservoir. Turn right and you will find a large barbecue and sitting out area next to the Upper Jubilee Reservoir.

Consult the final part of MacLehose trail section 6 to get back to Tsuen Wan by minibus. You could also backtrack this section to go back all the way to Tai Po Road, or end up in Kwai Chung. For details of this path, you may consult Magic Walk 32 (volume 2b).

* * * *

Down the slippery slope (page 77)

The MacLehose Trail

Section 6
Tai Po Road to Shing Mun Reservoir
Difficulty: Grade 1. Time Estimate: 2 hours; 4.6 km

Section Six provides an ideal opportunity for those who don't have the time or ability to handle more than a few relatively easy kilometres. The first part is a steady climb up a concrete path followed by an easy elevated walk along a good footpath, before a drop to Shing Mun Reservoir.

Public transport is even easier for this section as a bus route goes almost directly to the start and a minibus is a short walk away at the end. This section can be easily completed in half a day. The first part of the section is pleasant but has no really interesting views. Your hard work is rewarded, however, once you climb up onto Smuggler's Ridge to look out over western Kowloon. This is a great introduction to hiking for the hesitant or inexperienced.

Taking a breather near Smuggler's Ridge

The MacLehose Trail

1. ROUTE DETAILS

Kowloon Reservoir to Smuggler's Ridge

Coming from Section Five follow the previous directions onto Golden Hill Road. If arriving by bus from Sham Shui Po, you should get off when the bus stops its steady climb along Tai Po Road. There is a pedestrian walkway over the road at that point; the bus stop is called Shek Lei Pui Reservoir. Walk north on Tai Po Road for 2 mins until you see a sign on the left for Golden Hill Road and a board with a map of Kam Shan (Golden Hill) Country Park. You may well see very tame macaques by the litter bins at the side of this road before you get to the reservoir. These monkeys are used to humans, but it would be unwise to approach them or provoke them. If you don't interfere with them they'll leave you alone.

You'll thread between Kowloon Reservoir on your right and the much smaller Byewash Reservoir on your left. The road then starts to climb away from the reservoirs. Shortly, you'll see an

Hong Kong harbour as seen from Kam Shan

The MacLehose Trail

Jubilee Reservoir with Tsuen Wan in the background

emergency telephone on your left by one of the ubiquitous shelters. On the first part of the trail, the concrete access road goes past a number of family trails and jogging trails on its climb north to Smuggler's Ridge. The whole place was deserted when I was there midweek. It's a good place to rest up after finishing Section Five; there are toilets and picnic areas around here. Don't go down the right trail marked Kam Shan Family Walk (after about 1km); continue straight on. Soon you'll see the end of Smuggler's Ridge rise up in front of you. As the road begins to drop, ignore the concrete road on the right and also the unmarked footpath that rises up Smuggler's Ridge on your right. This is an alternative if you want a more strenuous climb as it meets the MacLehose Trail after going over the very top of Smuggler's Ridge.

Smuggler's Ridge to Shung Mun Reservoir

Further down the road, take a footpath marked with the, by

The MacLehose Trail

now, familiar hiker. After a short rise, a fairly flat ridge now heads northwest for about a kilometre. The estate below you is Kwai Chung. When I walked this section, Home Ownership Scheme flats were being built on the small area of flat ground that remained between the hills and the urban area. There are good vistas of Tsing Yi Island and much of the west of Hong Kong from the ridge. You'll pass over a little footbridge near this point, then head up a small climb. The ridge drops away to your left so watch your footwork around here. Turning north around the corner of Smuggler's Ridge the trail starts to drop and the more northern Sections Seven and Eight come into view. You should be able to pick out Needle Hill ahead and Tai Mo Shan if they aren't engulfed in clouds. The Shing Mun Reservoirs also come into view at this point.

After this pass, you'll come to a concrete tunnel entrance with 'Shaftsbury Avenue' inscribed on it. This is an entryway to a subterranean system of hideouts once used by the British Army. See Living History Section below. Watch the steps here as some of them are quite badly eroded. You exit to a large open picnic area. Walking across, you will find an information board and

Looking down at Lower Shing Mun Reservoir from the top of the dam!

emergency telephone. Walk past this onto the road to the edge of the dam. Section Seven is right, the minibus to Tsuen Wan is left (see details in Transport Section below).

2. FEATURES OF THE ROUTE

Kam Shan Country Park is largely the product of a reforestation programme completed after World War II. It's in its infancy as a natural habitat - a fact that's apparent from the small trees on the first part of the trail. It's one of the most well-used of all the country parks, despite being one of the smallest. The reservoirs here were completed in the early twentieth century and are minute engineering projects compared to the later High Island and Plover Cove Reservoirs. Indeed the whole area seems miniature compared to some of the more dramatic sights on the trail, but it's perfect for anyone looking for tranquillity in pleasant surroundings. Indeed, the lower part of the walk is like a stroll through a public park.

It's not until you climb onto Smuggler's Ridge that you begin to get a sense of the challenge of the wilds, although, even here, with modern estates butting up to the foothills of the mountains, you know you're just a stone's throw away from the city.

In the contest between the real estate developers and Mother Nature it seems the former are creeping little by little to victory. Here the trail comes the closest to the container port of Kwai Chung. Although it's an eyesore, Kwai Chung is of vast importance to Southern China. In 1988 Hong Kong eclipsed New York and Rotterdam as the world's largest container port. Since then, Singapore briefly overtook Hong Kong, but by 1993, Kwai Chung had regained first place with 9.2 million TEUs (20-ft equivalent units). Estimated throughput in 1994 was 11 million TEUs spread over 8 container terminals. Hong Kong acts as the main outlet for the industrial products not only of Hong Kong but of the whole of the developed and industrialised southern Chinese seaboard.

The MacLehose Trail

Living History –

World War II Fortifications in Kam Shan Country Park

The innocuous look of the entrance bearing the cryptic name 'Shaftsbury Avenue' found towards the end of this section belies the drama of its violent history.

The entrance leads through a maze of underground fortifications that were built as a defence against the Japanese during World War II - the main line was from Gin Drinker's Lane in the east to Shatin. When Japanese troops advanced from the north in December 1941, the Shing Mun redoubt under Needle Hill was the kingpin in the defence. Fortifications fell soon after it was taken. Hours after the fierce hand-to-hand battle was won by the Japanese, the whole of the Kowloon peninsula was in enemy hands. The pathways in the system were named after various places in London, which must have been a source of comfort to the beleaguered British troops.

3. TRANSPORT AND OTHER DETAILS

Getting There

There is a car park just north of the start of Piper's Hill.

The best bus to catch is #72 from Tai Kok Tsui. Take the MTR to Mongkok and take the exit that leads you west along Argyle Street to the bus stop. Get off the bus on Tai Po Road (ask the driver for Kam Shan). If you see the reservoir on your left, you've gone too far.

Times: The first bus from Tai Kok Tsui is at 6.00 am, the last returning there from Tai Wok Estate at 11.00p.m.

Frequency: Every 18-30 minutes.

The taxi ride from Shamshuipo MTR is, of course, quicker and will cost less than $20.

Getting Away

At the end of the trail take minibus #82 to the centre of Tsuen

Wan and from there you can get the MTR. On Sundays minibus #94 also runs from the same pick-up point near Pineapple Dam at Shing Mun. To get to the stop, which is just below Jubilee Reservoir Visitor Centre, take a left on the road you've exited onto at the end of the section. The road goes past the southern tip of the reservoir. There's a helpful sign showing all the various walks and jogging trails round the reservoir as well as local landmarks. Ignore the road that U turns left for Lei Muk Shue Estate. Go past the Ranger's Centre and you'll eventually see the terminus in front of the Visitor Centre.

The Visitor Centre has interesting displays about the nature and history of the area. The 3D model of the local flora and fauna gives you a good idea of where you will walk on the next section. Check it out if you arrive by minibus to walk Section Seven.

Accommodation

There are no campsites or hostels on this section. There is a refreshment kiosk at the minibus #82 terminus underneath the Visitor Centre.

* * * *

Overlooking Shing Mun Reservoir after a bush fire

Section 7
Shing Mun Reservoir to Lead Mine Pass

Difficulty: Grade 2. Time Estimate: 3 hours (4 hours if descending to Tai Po Kau/Shing Mun at the end of the route). Distance: 6.2 km (11.2 km to Tai Po Kau/Shing Mun).

If you want a bridge between the grade one and three sections of the trail, this is ideal. It features a couple of easier sections on roads and some stiff but relatively short climbs that will get your legs and heart pumping. It has the benefit of being reached quite quickly from Tsuen Wan but offers quite an exciting and wild climb up the unusual Needle Hill, an excellent place to get a panorama of Hong Kong. It also offers a clamber down to Lead Mine Pass, which is good fun. If you're not going onto Section Eight, you must add on about 5 kilometres by walking down to Tai Po Kau or in the other direction back to Shing Mun.

Two old friends meet during the charity hike

The MacLehose Trail

Trail walkers descend from Needle Hill

1. ROUTE DETAILS

Shing Mun Reservoir to the road from Needle Hill Summit

This walk starts from the southern tip of Shing Mun (Jubilee)

The MacLehose Trail

Looking north towards Lead Mine Pass

Reservoir in Shing Mun Country Park. From the end of Section Six, you'll hit the concrete road at the side of the picnic area as you come off Smuggler's Ridge. The road goes right and Section Seven is signposted this way. If you've made it up from Tsuen Wan by minibus you'll approach this road from the west. Simply keep going past the picnic area on your right as the main road goes around the corner. (See Transport Section)

You'll approach the main dam on this road. (The smaller dam on the opposite side of the reservoir, above the minibus #82 stop is known as Pineapple Dam). Section Seven actually starts across the main dam. The rocky valley on your right is the start of lower Shing Mun Reservoir. Lion Rock and Beacon Hill rise majestically in the background. This is quite a popular place for

The MacLehose Trail

the younger Chinese to hang out, as I discovered on a public holiday, perhaps because the scenery is so magnificent.

Over the dam the concrete road forks, with the trail going right. Very soon you'll notice steps leading away from the road under a big wooden sign that indicates the trail. The climb here is quite steep as steps lead out to a broader earth path. On the hillside of this initial climb, you can see lots of erosion from all the mining that used to be done around here. Along the path to Needle Hill there are good views of Tsuen Wan behind you. The construction on the bridge from the island of Tsing Yi, that will connect Kowloon to the new airport on Lantau Island, Chek Lap Kok, is proceeding rapidly. This enormous project will alter, quite radically, this particular view of Hong Kong.

The path drops down after about a kilometre from the start and then goes over a small plateau as Needle Hill comes into view. The path here is slippery when wet and is also badly eroded.

Between Grassy Hill and Needle Hill

It looks quite steep but don't worry, there are steps. To the left, the upper part of Shing Mun Reservoir is far beneath you as Tai Mo Shan rises behind.

The triangulation point on the top of Needle Hill is one of the best vantage points in all of Hong Kong. Shatin, built around what is now the Shing Mun River Channel, is on your right, overshadowed by the easily recognisable Lion Rock and Beacon Hill. You can see in front of you the concrete road you'll pick up after coming down the hill. Be careful of the drop towards the reservoir on your left - stay away as it's quite steep. Also be careful of your footing going down - there are concrete steps but they may be quite slippy after rain. Take it slowly one step at a time and be sure of your footwork (we were actually overtaken by a cheerful and sprightly old-age pensioner on this part of the route because we were being so careful).

Road from the bottom of Needle Hill to Lead Mine Pass

After joining this road at the bottom of the climb, carry on in a northerly direction. First pass an open area with a gateway to Shatin on your right. You continue on the road unless using this as an escape route: it's about 3km to Shatin from this point or about an hour's walk.(This trail can become tricky if it has been raining, though). To carry on, follow the road through a quiet wooded area to a split where you go right (left takes you back to Shing Mun Reservoir). The road from Needle Hill to here is broad and flat but after this point, it starts to climb towards Grassy Hill. At another split, there's a left turn which is, in fact, a short cut to Lead Mine Pass (also signposted for a campsite and Tai Po). Bear right here. Climb out of the woods through a strange boulder-strewn landscape with charred stick-like trees at the roadside. The hills to Shatin stretch away to your right. In drifting mist or clouds this place assumes quite an eerie atmosphere. You bend round a corner and the triangulation point on top of Grassy Hill comes into view. At this point look out for the

The MacLehose Trail

Escape route to Shatin and Fo Tan

trail, which is marked left as you turn off the main road onto what looks like a minor footpath. You can see the pass below you and Tai Po and the northern New Territories on the right. The forests of Shing Mun Country Park are on your right as you descend.

WARNING: After heavy rain this path is very steep and slippery. Good boots are a must and a walking stick is very helpful. You pass through charred trees and parts of the path may be covered with large grassy plants. Watch your step: I went down on my backside at least once and if you're not careful you'll end up mud skiing to the bottom! Try to place your feet on rocks or roots and take small steps. It can put a fair amount of strain on your knees. It's best to have both hands free to use a stick or to steady yourself on trees or rocks.

Exit at the bottom onto the road opposite a picnic site, then go <u>left</u>. *If you wish to go back via Tai Po Kau you must go right here*. There is a staggered junction straight on down the hill on the right where the trail is signposted. An immediate left will take you either back down the side of Shing Mun Reservoir or back towards Needle Hill. You go past a management centre to a

Most of Section Seven is a concrete path

large open area with toilets, emergency telephone shelters and, should you ever require it, a helipad. Section Eight is marked by a wooden gate off the main road. If you follow the main road you'll go back to the southern end of Shing Mun reservoir to the minibus stop. This is about another 5 km.

2. FEATURES OF THE ROUTE

Going up Needle Hill then Grassy Hill you are roughly halfway between the eastern and western extremes of the New Territories. This walk gives you a good idea of the two opposing facets of the New Territories, with the surreal blend of high-rise, high-tech office building and housing estates, in stark contrast to the timeless landscape of the ancient, wild hills. If you pick a good day with clear skies you should be able to see Tsuen Wan, Lantau, Shatin and the Ma On Shan range of hills behind it, Tolo Harbour, the northern New Territories, Tai Po and Tai Mo Shan, all on this one comparatively short walk. The government's new town programme has changed this once very quiet rural backwater completely. Once a neglected agricultural area, the New Territories now act as Hong Kong's bedroom. Despite the questionable aesthetics of the developments, the programme has been amazingly successful in soaking up the colony's excess population. Tai Po and Shatin are virtual overnight success stories. The former has an annual population growth rate of over 10 percent and may grow to swallow the nearby traditional village of Hong Lok Yuen. Shatin, previously a cluster of fishing dwellings with a population of a few thousand, shot up in the 1960's and now houses over half a million people. Its population could reach a million in the next few years, placing greater stress on the surrounding natural environment.

Shing Mun Reservoir, often known as Jubilee Reservoir, was finished in 1936 and was named to mark the silver anniversary of the coronation of England's King George V. At the time it was the biggest dam in Hong Kong but now only holds a tiny fraction of the water that's in Plover Cove and High Island. The smaller dam on the western shore of the reservoir is known as Pineapple Dam, recalling the history of the area. In the eighteenth century the Shing Mun valley was settled by Hakka peasants who lived

Jubilee Reservoir as seen from Grassy Hill

The MacLehose Trail

The last 500m to the top are the hardest

in several villages. The relationship between these Hakkas and residents of neighbouring Tsuen Wan deteriorated in the nineteenth century and resulted in conflict as the Tsuen Wan villagers wanted to charge Shing Mun Hakkas for going through their area to sell pineapples at market.

The first main climb up Needle Hill gives you a chance to observe at first hand the effects of mining, which left this hill gashed with large scars of bare orange earth and heavy erosion.

Living History – Mining at Needle Hill

Needle Hill mine originally produced lead which petered out in the late nineteenth century. This was succeeded by the discovery of tungsten ore, the mining of which ceased when the Japanese occupied the New Territories. After the Japanese left in the 1940's, the mine reopened, and tungsten became the main source of income for the villagers. Production ceased in the 1960's as lower international prices and the increasing cost of local labour

The MacLehose Trail

sounded the death knell of the industry, leaving only this unusually-shaped bleak hill as its epitaph.

The Shing Mun area has long been of military significance in the history of Hong Kong. During World War II, the British forces suffered defeat at the hands of the Japanese, who overran their

The descent to Lead Mine Pass can be hazardous on a foggy day

The MacLehose Trail

subterranean fortifications in the area. There was a fort here as early as the seventeenth century occupied by Manchurian forces (Shing Mun means literally 'fort gate'), who had recently defeated marauding pirates.

3. TRANSPORT
Getting There

Get off the MTR at Tsuen Wan and find minibus #82 (it should have a sign for Jubilee Reservoir on the front). This will take you to the Visitor Centre at Jubilee Dam. From here follow the road uphill away from the Visitor Centre and go past a Country Parks Ranger Centre. Ignore the right split in the road to Lei Muk Shue Estate. The road goes past the southern tip of the reservoir then rejoins it at a large picnic site. You'll see a map on your right at the picnic site showing you that this is the start of Section Seven. Follow the road round the reservoir to the open area where Section Six joins it.

Getting Away

You can finish either where you started at Shing Mun Visitor Centre or go on to Tai Po Kau and catch bus #72 to Tai Po or Kowloon (Tai Kok Tsui). For directions see access route details at the start of Section Eight. Follow the directions in reverse.

Accommodation

There is a designated campsite with toilets (but no refreshments) at Lead Mine Pass at the end of this section.

* * * *

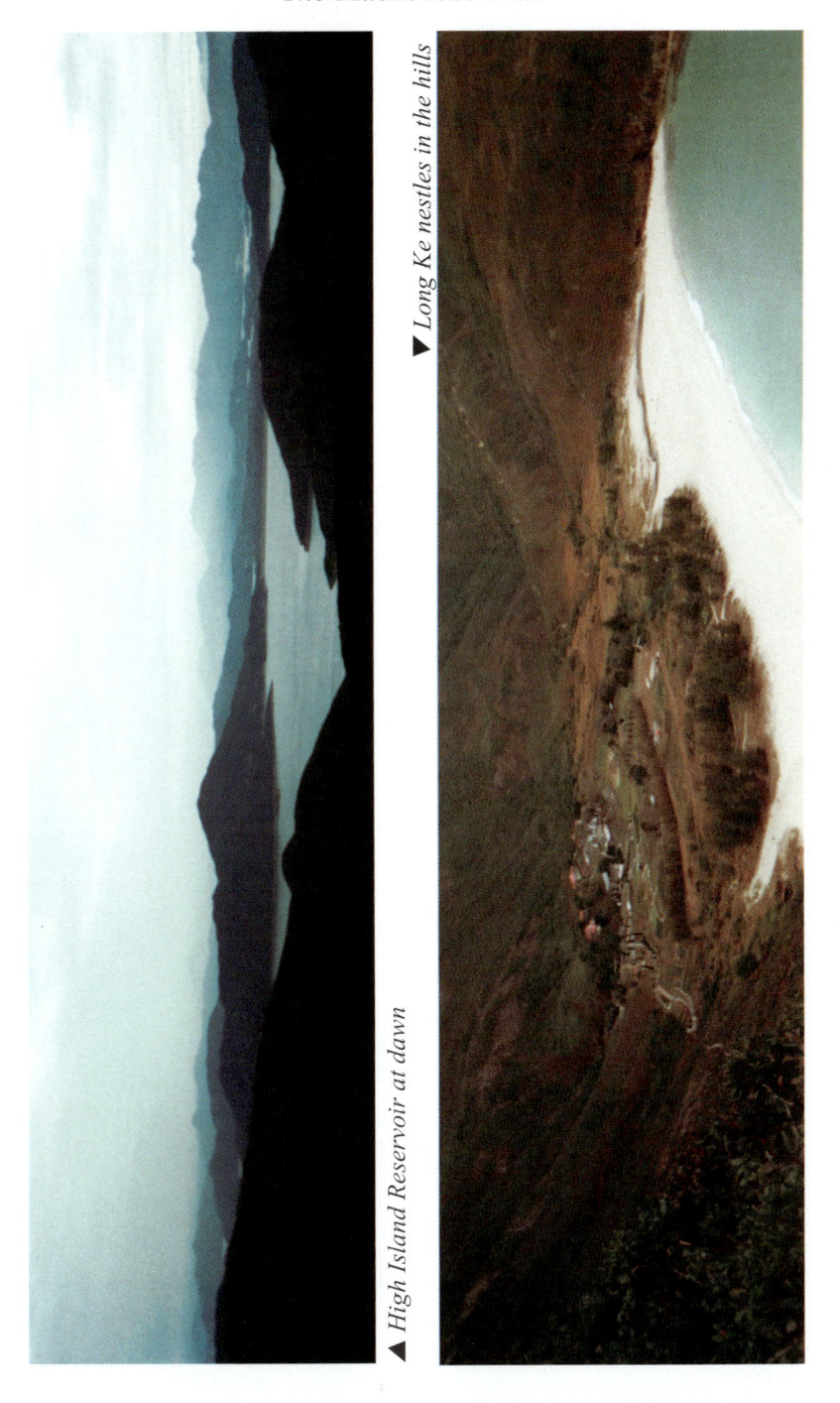

The MacLehose Trail

◀ High Island Reservoir at dawn

▼ Long Ke nestles in the hills

The MacLehose Trail

▶ Ham Tin Wan and Mong Yue Kok

◀ Sai Wan Beach on a weekday

The MacLehose Trail

▶ *Tsang Pang Kok Peninsula*

▼ *Sai Wan with Sharp Peak Range*

The MacLehose Trail

Spring blossoms on Stage 3

Hebe Haven and Rocky Bay (Stage 4)

The MacLehose Trail

Bougainville near Siu Lek Yuen (Excursion 1)

The forest trail near Tai Po Kau (Excursion 3)

The MacLehose Trail

Tai Po Kau and Ma On Shan

Sek Kong Valley

The MacLehose Trail

Near Ho Pui after a rainstorm (Stage 9)

The MacLehose Trail

View from Stage 9 to Kadoorie Farm and Lam Kam Road

View of Hong Kong Island from Excursion 4

The MacLehose Trail

Excursion 3 (MacLehose 7)
Fo Tan Station to Grassy Hill

The walk from Fo Tan station to Grassy Hill is about 3.5- 5km depending on the route chosen. It can be managed in 2-3 hours in order to join the MacLehose Trail. The alternative Cove Hill excursion is longer and one needs to allow for at least three hours to enjoy it. Degree of difficulty: 3 for both excursions, and if descent along Cove Hill is included: 4.

A great stroll! That is normally how we announce the excursion to the members of our walking club ahead of time. It is hard to imagine when you pull into Fo Tan KCR station that such a lovely valley is half an hour away hidden behind all the ugly factory skyscrapers. The dirty air produced by manufacturing and incessant traffic of container trucks and public transport is completely at odds with the fresh air of the countryside.

When you leave the station on the north-western side, turn left (direction Sui Wo Court/Shatin Galleria) towards the elevated highway called Fo Tan Road which you must follow to the end of the factory district. To do that, you should cross the footbridge and turn right towards the hills that are barely discernible in the distance. Just follow the channel that cuts the factory district in two (Fo Tan Toad is on the right side of it). After about 1km turn left into Kwai Tei Road. You will find a small recreation area laid out immediately on the right. The start of our real walk is here towards the hills.

The water that runs into the channel you have followed comes from a little stream that we shall follow for part of our hike. There are steps a mere 150m from Kwai Tei Garden that brings you to the next level overlooking a bus parking lot of Citibus. There is another set of stair 20m ahead on your right which will lead you to the countryside we are about to visit.

The path is concrete and good most of the first half of our

The MacLehose Trail

hike. The steps on the left after 200m lead to Kwai Tei New Village; although the old maps give the impressions that you can get up Grassy Hill this way, I would rather you do not try it. The second (more crude) steps on the left are for the benefit of the technicians of China Light & Power. After a few hundred meters, you will come to a bridge that is used to cross the brook in the rainy season. Usually you can cross along the concrete path that runs under the bridge. The path continues and becomes a bit steeper on the other side.

You have to take a decision at this point how much time you intend to invest on the walk. You will have noticed by now that the valley is very pronounced with hills on both sides and has a definite end to it. It is thus easy to understand that you will make one or more contour walks. You pass two tiny villages and at the first one near light pole VA26332, you should take a left turn (option 1) if you have a modest amount of time or energy, and turn right (option 2) if you have lots of either.

Let's take option 1 first: you need to take the left turn every

Ho Lek Pui hidden in the bushes

The MacLehose Trail

Ma On Shan and Whitehead (across the water)

time you see a fork. Ignore the one path that leads down to the water. The two hamlets Yiu Dau Ping and Wo Sheng Tun (each less than 10 houses and thirty souls each including dogs) should stay on your right. After a few hundred meters, you will come to a tiny footbridge that crosses the brook once more. You will notice that the real, steep trail that used to exist at this point (on the other side) has been transformed into a proper, concrete footpath courtesy of the Shatin District Board: 'Construction of Footpath at Shan Mei Village'. It passes a tangerine orchard on the right, a lovely sight at the end of the year and up to Chinese New Year. This is big business for the Chinese. Follow the main trail at all points from this crossing (the last time you cross the brook); the trail continues to lead uphill at about 15-20% angles.

When you have walked another 800m from the last bridge, the trail levels off a bit and the concrete path stops. Ignore the left turn down into the fields. This is good point to take a breather before the next rougher stretch. There is a faint trail into the bushes on the right with a sign Au Pui Wan (the name of a deserted village that you will encounter if you go to Grassy Hill). The trail turns into a real path and rapidly becomes steeper again. You have to be quite careful on the next stretch. There are two trails on the right that you could easily miss. Ignore the first one which leads

The MacLehose Trail

Fo Tan seen from near Grassy Hill

to a graveside where there is a stone marked with red paint. The second one is found where the stepping stones end and where there is a clearing. Turn right here for the shortest road to the top of a crest. You will soon be out in the open; the path passes through bamboo and grass that often grows to a man's height.

However, if you want to go to Grassy Hill (option 3 - see below), you must continue straight uphill at the 'clearing'.

When following option 1, you will see that there is an excellent path without undergrowth as soon as you reach the crest. The reason is that the path from Grassy Hill down into the forest joins here. The view towards Fo Tan is enchanting and very contrasting. The hills on the other side of Shatin Cove and the Shing Mun River Channel are truly magnificent. Turn right towards the trees. The path in the forest is easy to follow and well-travelled.

Once you leave the forest, the path twist and turns, then crosses another brook. You have to climb the last little stretch on the other side to the concrete road built by the army. If you turn left (see

The MacLehose Trail

map), you will reach the main hardened road that leads to Leadmine Pass. If you choose to stay on the excursion, turn right. After 300m there is a fork; take the right, high road. It ends after a few hundred meters as a concrete road (at a helicopter pad), but the actual path continues. There is an excellent, very wide view over Tolo Harbour, Whitehead Detention Camp, Ma On Shan and the Chinese University of Hong Kong.

Cove Hill is right in front of you. If you want to have the best view of this walk, by all means climb this hill and descend on the other side. But I must warn you that part of the trail down becomes very difficult. The easiest path is where the trail meets the second forest on the left. The path down is on the right. People practising 'orienteering' and/or the Hash House Harriers have attached plastic strands to the undergrowth. This path tends to be overgrown as well, but becomes quite clear after the first hiker passes through the grass if you are with a group.

It is a contour walk. When you have descended about 50m in height and 200m in a straight line, turn right and stay on the contour of the hill. It passes along the hills, then turns left when it meets another faint trail and leads down in a straight line along

Escape from the urban jungle

the crest of a little hill that sticks out into the valley.

You will land on the concrete path below. You will notice a small hamlet to the right in the valley from where the path is coming. This is called Ho Lek Pui (see below). Once you hit the path, turn left. It becomes now an easy descent through two more orchards and the two villages that we passed uphill. You will arrive at the trail you took before after about 1km, from where it is just another 30 mins back to the station. The descent down is, of course, much faster than the ascent. There are several restaurants that cater to the working class along the (already mentioned) channel in Fo Tan factory district that are competitive in price and where the service is friendly.

Option 2: When you take the right turn, you will be following the path you are taking on the way back of option 1 (see above) but in the opposite direction. It is about 1km to the hamlet of Ho Lek Pui which consists of just one extended farmhouse. You will be welcomed from afar by the sound of several alert barking dogs. The trail passes in front of the farm. Where there is a split in the path, turn left. The path occasionally becomes indistiguishable which means that it is not without adventure. If you end up near a two-shed hamlet that appears to be deserted in the daytime, you are too high and have to descend one level to come back to the trail. You will end up near Shan Mei Village from where you have to turn right and join option 1 or even option 3 (see below). The rest is the same. Option 2 adds 1.5km to your excursion.

Option 3: When you reach the 'clearing' (see above), continue straight uphill. This is now possible as someone has reclaimed this trail back from nature. I got lost here a few times in the past. There is another split in the trail after about 200m; you will see a marked stone with blue paint at this exact point. Turn right and follow this trail until you reach the main trail already described.

By turning right you will join option 1 after a short walk. But if you want to reach Grassy Hill, you need to turn left.

The MacLehose Trail

Near Shan Mei Tsuen

There are power pylons overhead after about 200m; there is a path on the left after another 100m which you should ignore as you might get hopelessly lost. Continue in the same direction that shortly reaches a brook. The path continues on the other side across the rocks and reaches the deserted village of Au Pui Wan. It is called Shek Lau Tung on other maps (but unfortunately, the maps are not very accurate).

The path continues on the other side of the village and slowly winds itself through another forest until it reaches Grassy Hill. It ends about 300m from the top to the south. If you have no intention of following the MacLehose Trail from here on, the easiest way to end your excursion is to walk downhill along the concrete road to the next crossroads, where you should turn right in the direction of Lead Mine Pass. At the next fork (about 500m), turn left towards Jubilee (Shing Mun) Reservoir. You will enjoy this leisure and easy walk through the trees, even on a hot and sunny day where the foliage will protect yoy from the penetrating rays of the sun. You may even have enough energy to visit the Arboretum, i.e. scientific tree garden found a short distance from here on the right.

It is another 2km on foot from here to the minibus stop just under Pineapple Dam. There are often delays in the service late

The MacLehose Trail

in the afternoon, and it is almost as easy to walk down to the Shing Mun tunnel exit another 500m down the road from where a great number of buses will whisk you back to town. I have done this entire walk (including option 2) in less than four hours on a rainy day. Since you are probably unfamiliar with any of the territory covered, count on spending 5-6 hours to reach Tsuen Wan from Fo Tan. If you include travelling time, you should be prepared to spend the better part of a day altogether, certainly if you wish to enjoy the stunning views.

* * * *

On the other side of the hill, the view north to Tai Po

The MacLehose Trail

Section 8
Lead Mine Pass to Route Twisk

Difficulty: Grade 2. Time Estimate: 4 hours (for the actual route; add one hour for access from nearest point of public transport). Distance: 9.7 km (14-15 km including walk from nearest public transport)

Now it's time to conquer Tai Mo Shan, Hong Kong's tallest mountain. There are panoramic views of Yuen Long and the new airport project between Lantau and Tsing Yi Islands. You can start out in quiet woods at either Tai Po or Shing Mun and after covering the summit, drop down to Route Twisk from where it's a ten-minute bus ride to Tsuen Wan.

This is one of the more difficult grade two sections even though the majority of it is on a road. It is ideal if you want a greater challenge than grade two but feel grade three may be too taxing. It features a couple of quite strenuous climbs although neither should have you using your hands - the first is largely stepped and the second is up a very twisty road.

It's a good half day's trip. There is no place to buy food so

The path leading north from Tai Mo Shan to Kadoorie Farm

it's best to bring at least some fruit or snacks. There's a Youth Hostel as you descend Tai Mo Shan, which would be an ideal breaking point for an overnight stop without having to carry camping gear; then you can go on to Section Nine the next day. You would be well advised to pick a particularly fine day as Ma On Shan is often shrouded in mist, thwarting your chance of seeing some of the best views in Hong Kong. Of all the times I've been walking on or near this mountain I've only once had a completely clear view of it.

Tai Po Kau forest trail (near Lead Mine Pass)

1. **ROUTE DETAILS**

Lead Mine Pass to the start of Tai Mo Shan Road

There are two ways to get to Lead Mine Pass – from either Tai Po Road to the north or the base of Shing Mun Reservoir to the south. Take bus #72 and get off at Tai Po Kau. If you have time, you might want to start off from the Chinese University at Shatin to take in its splendid spacious atmosphere. From either

The MacLehose Trail

place you can find the road heading southwest from Tai Po Road through Tung Tsai Yuen. Go past the Country Park Management Centre on your left, and go right at the next three junctions to get to Lead Mine Pass. It's about 6km from the stop near Tai Po Kau Village and 10km from the Chinese University to the start of the route.

If you are coming from the south, take minibus #82 from Tsuen Wan to the last stop at Jubilee Reservoir. Take the road to the immediate left. Go uphill for five minutes then take a right up a road with a barrier over it, opposite a car park. This is a quiet wooded walk past the west side of the reservoir with Needle Hill (across the water) on your right. Go right at the first T junction, then left at the next two splits which should be signposted for Lead Mine Pass. I approached this way when walking the trail on a very hot and humid summer day and it took about an hour to get to the start of Section Eight. It's about 6km.

The start of this section is a big open area with shelters, a toilet and an emergency phone. The trail is obviously marked under a wooden gate. There is also a helipad further down the

Kadoorie Farm lies on the north slope of Tai Mo Shan

The MacLehose Trail

Hong Kong's most spectacular waterfalls north of Tai Mo Shan

road. When I was there it was being used by police who had just completed Section Eight as a training run in full uniform and were being shipped by air back to base! Go through the trees - after a few minutes there's a great lookout over Tai Po to the north with the Pat Sin range of mountains behind it and Plover Cove Reservoir and Tolo Harbour stretching into the blue eastern haze.

After about a 30 minute climb you emerge above the tree line. You will thread your way through boulders and then the trail levels out, with a view of the grassy plateau in front of you and a small rise in front of Ma On Shan in the distance. Glance back whilst climbing to the plateau over the rocks and see if you can pick out the marker on Grassy Hill and the various peaks above Kowloon (the distinctive Lion Rock is always easiest). If it's clear, you can see the Bank of China on Hong Kong Island. Once on the plateau, the trail narrows in places and goes over rocks where there's no obvious path. You should always be able to pick up the trail after a few minutes.

Ahead you can see a plateau. Again pick your way over this and after a few minutes the plateau drops down. The trail leading to the start of the road should be clearly visible.

Tai Mo Shan Road to Route Twisk

At the start of the road, signposts indicate a good escape route on the footpath via a waterfall at Ng Tung Chai Village.

If there's bad weather you could take this path to Lam Kam Road and catch bus #64K to Tai Po KCR Station. Twisk is 6.2km from the sign. Another possibility is to pick up the path to the experimental Kadoorie farm, named after its wealthy benefactor brothers, whose aim is to experiment with agriculture so as to benefit local farmers. Although a permit is needed to ascend Tai Mo Shan through the farm, one isn't needed if descending (look out for Kwun Yam Shan on your left as you descend).

The road twists up the southern face and from a couple of points the very distinctive features of the watery fields behind Yuen Long can be seen, with the military runway of Sek Kong in the foreground. The smaller steep-sided and deeply-ravined moun-

Fire-tree in full bloom at Ng Tung Chai Tsuen

The MacLehose Trail

Towards Tai Mo Shan at Kadoorie Farm

tain ranges that rise abruptly from the flat valley floor north of the runway are the two ranges that make up Lam Tsuen Country Park. You'll pass a small transmitting station when you arrive at a T junction, then turn south to go past the main radio station. Tsuen Wan should come into view before you turn the corner and go down the south side of Tai Mo Shan on a series of sharp hairpins.

It's impossible to get lost as you simply follow the road to Route Twisk. Just after a checkpoint on the road there's a left for the Youth Hostel that's not very clearly marked. This is the limit of access by private car to this side of the hill, but since there's a car park, it's a possible drop-off or pick-up point. On the right are good spots to have lunch whilst admiring the Yuen Long scenery. Before coming to Route Twisk, you might like to drop in at the Tai Mo Shan Visitor Centre, though this seemed a little short on information about the area.

Turn right at the main road towards the #51 bus stop back to Tsuen Wan. The start of Section Nine is opposite, by the big Yuen Long sign post.

2. FEATURES OF THE ROUTE

The construction of Jubilee Reservoir in the 1930's destroyed a total of eight Hakka villages. It's hard to imagine the vanished shadows of the homes of generations of Hakka farmers under the reservoir's placid turquoise waters as you make your way to Lead Mine Pass. Most of the villagers were resettled in the Kam Tin area at great expense to the government - the Hakkas originally had forestry rights to 40 % of what is now Shing Mun Country Park.

The rocky plateau at the beginning of this section is unique on the trail - go up on a misty day and you'd think you were in the north of England rather than Hong Kong. Huge granite boulders are scattered about, creating an interesting contrast to Ma On Shan, which has a more alpine feel. The ascent here is very gradual and it's not at all obvious you're approaching the highest mountain in the territory. Ancient tea terraces are in evidence all over on the plateau and have often been subjected to land movement, giving rise to interesting shapes. They are so old, their origin pre-dates written records.

Looking down on Tsing Yi, the small island off Tsuen Wan, you can't help feeling ambivalent towards the effects of development on the island. Once the home of excellent swimming beaches, it then became the repository of heavy industry, including oil depots, and is now an essential part of the airport core project. This over-development may have destroyed the quality of life for some inhabitants, but it has also allowed some to sell their land at a large profit and has made many local people rich.

Without a doubt, the new airport is an integral part of the boom in development stemming from the creation of free economic zones on the southern coast of China, as well as being a great feat of engineering in itself. The Lantau fixed crossing that was under construction when this book was written will be the longest of its kind in the world. It can be seen as part of a bigger process in the unparalleled rapid growth that will conceivably turn the whole area between Hong Kong and Canton into a vast urban megalopolis by the middle of the next century.

The unusually named Route Twisk is an acronym of Tsuen Wan and Sek Kong (T.W.S.K.), the two towns that it connects.

3. TRANSPORT AND ACCOMMODATION
Getting There
— To Tai Po Kau

Take bus #72 (not 72x which goes through Lion Rock Tunnel to Shatin), from Mongkok (or the now defunct Tai Kok Tsui Ferry Pier). For further directions and times see Transport under Section Six. Get off at the stop near Tai Po Kau village.

— To Jubilee (Shing Mun) Reservoir

Take the MTR to Tsuen Wan then minibus #82 to the last stop. Follow the above directions. Full details of minibus #82 are in Section Seven.

Getting Away

Bus #51 from Kam Tin on Route Twisk takes you back to Tsuen Wan Ferry Pier. Get off just after coming into Tsuen Wan on top of a flyover then drop down to the MTR.

Times:		
	First bus from Tsuen Wan	6.30 a.m.
	Last bus from Tsuen Wan	11.20 p.m.
	First bus from Kam Tin	5.40 a.m.
	Last bus from Kam Tin	10.25 p.m.

* * * *

The MacLehose Trail

Section 9
Route Twisk to Tin Fu Tsai

Difficulty: Grade 1. Time Estimate: 3-4 hours; 6.3 km (Add 8 km or another 2 hours to reach public transport from Tin Fu Tsai)

The great bulk of Tai Mo Shan slopes down towards Route Twisk and joins the gentle wooded hills of Tai Lam Country Park and Section Nine.

This walk combines interesting views over Yuen Long with an easy hike through shaded woodland. The gradients are a little easier than those on Sections One and Six, the earlier grade one sections. An added advantage is the dappled shade of the trees on either side of the trail, a real plus on a hot summer day. The more open Sections One and Six can be extremely hot between May and October.

The start is only a 15-minute bus ride up Route Twisk from Tsuen Wan. At the end of this section, there's no immediate public transport, so you must take a footpath south and pick up a bus at Tsing Lung Tau back to Tsuen Wan.

The first steep incline from Route Twisk

The MacLehose Trail

1. ROUTE DETAILS

Route Twisk to Tin Fu Tsai Campsite

After taking bus #51 from Tsuen Wan, you'll pass the Country Management Centre on your left (until July 1997, it will be flying a Union Jack). Get off at the first stop after this, and walk back a few metres towards the centre. Go down the road to the right of it. There's a signboard with maps just before the centre.

The path is obvious and easy most of the way, as it follows a private concrete road that provides access for the rangers to the eastern part of Tai Lam Country Park. Continue on this road, ignoring signs for Chuen Lung and Pat Shek. There are a couple of easy gradients to take you onto a plateau from where you get intermittent views over Tsuen Wan, and the Pat Heung and Sek Kong area to Yuen Long. There are various paths on the right to Ho Pui Reservoir and the Kap Lung Nature Trail during the first half hour – the whole of Section Nine is on concrete road so

A break before the next descent on Stage 9

114

The MacLehose Trail

Near Ho Pui Reservoir

ignore these latter diversions.

After about half an hour, there's a hill to your right with a fire lookout building on it and small villages cradling beneath it. At the next split, the road left goes to Lin Fa Shan whilst you keep right to go down the left hand side of the small hill into more woods. Looking back, there are good views of Tai Mo Shan and of the mountain ranges behind the Lam Tsuen Valley. On the descent of the fire lookout hill, you get the first glimpse of the badly eroded mountains behind Tai Lam Chung Reservoir, bearing deep gashes of orange earth. You can also glimpse the southern seaboard to the left.

After going down into more woods, there are paths via the Ho Pui Reservoir to Lam Tsuen Valley, a useful escape route in bad weather. There are two splits in the road before the campsite: at the first, go left ignoring the right hairpin back to Ho Pui Reservoir, and at the second, go left by the newly constructed picnic area.

On the last stage, twist and descend down through more ma-

The MacLehose Trail

Sek Kong valley as seen from near Stage 9

ture woodland, which is quite enchanting on a sunny day. At the last T junction, take a right in front of the signboard and shelter, which you should reach after about an hour's walk. Left takes you to Tsing Lung Tau on the coast from where you can get a bus (see Transport Section). It's 8.4km or about two hours by foot. This is the easiest way back to Kowloon or Hong Kong if you aren't camping or continuing on to Section Ten.

The last kilometre or so takes you into a small wooded valley to Tin Fu Tsai Campsite in a quiet idyllic glade. This is, rather incongruously, the end of Section 9. Another possible escape route here is via the village of Tsing Fai Tong to Sham Tseng (signposted left a little while after the campsite). This takes you on a footpath through the village to the coast. You need to consult your map on this exit.

2. FEATURES OF THE ROUTE

Perhaps more than anywhere else on the MacLehose Trail, Section Nine shows the effects of deforestation and erosion caused

The MacLehose Trail

by brush fires, most often started by visitors to the country parks. These fires have left 'badlands' devoid of plant or animal life and it will take years of painstaking replanting to replace them. The most active period of deforestation was during the 1930's and 1940's, when the majority of native trees were felled for fuel by local residents – reckless behaviour which the government failed to take any action against whatsoever. Since the 1950's, a concerted effort has been made by he Country Parks Authority to reforest as big an area as possible, but they have been struggling against the man-made brush fires, as well as the erosion left by monsoons.

The deeper valleys that you pass through on this section and throughout the trail are usually the best preserved areas, whilst open hillsides have been struck by the ravages of deforestation. This in turn has destroyed the natural habitat for animals, and sadly, the larger indigenous mammals are no longer a common sight in Hong Kong's countryside. Gone are the days when leopards and tigers could be found in Hong Kong (which were seen as late as the 1950's), and many of the slopes were covered in

From Stage 9 to Sek Kong valley

Tai Lam Chung Reservoir

lush forest. The struggle to reforest and prevent forest fire is seen everywhere along this section, from roadside signs to the fire beaters propped up at various stations along the way.

Some estimates put the total land area burnt every year in forest fires at five per cent of the total area of Hong Kong. Quite often, over 1,000 fires are reported in a single year. It is a preventable problem: the camper or hiker must take responsibility and make sure to extinguish all campfires completely and never throw matches or cigarettes on the ground.

The whole of the area around Yuen Long was once the territory of the Tang Clan, but modern developers now own most of the land around here. The area's original charm is still very much apparent as you look out across the plain, the high rises incongruously jutting above the beautiful blue paddy fields.

Nestling at the foot of Kai Kong Leng mountain range is the ancient walled village of the Kam Tin, a mere speck in the distance.

In the foreground, the Sek Kong runway appears as a strip of

The MacLehose Trail

tarmac. This British Forces Air Base was once a 'tent city' for Vietnamese refugees, used as an overspill during their initial heavy influx. It has now been abandoned for this particular use, as mass breakouts by Vietnamese were frequent. It's now used by the Hong Kong Parachuting Club whom you may see in action if you hike this part of the route on a clear and windless Saturday or Sunday.

3. TRANSPORT AND ACCOMMODATION DETAILS

Getting There

Take bus #51 from Tuen Wan MTR up Route Twisk. Bus #51 leaves from the bridge on top of the MTR (going north on Tai Ho Road North). See route details in this section and transport details in Section Eight for further information.

Getting Away

There are two ways to leave the trail and cut back south to the coast, as well as back to Tsuen Wan. They are both detailed in the route details. The first is the T-junction before Tin Fu Tsai Campsite, taking you to Tsing Lung Tau, and the second is the footpath leading to Sham Tseng just after the campsite. There are countless minibuses plying their trade between Castle Peak Road and Tsuen Wan MTR and even Mongkok, but if you prefer buses, then the following information is useful:

Bus #52X From Tuen Mun to Sham Shui Po, calling at Tsing Lung Tau and Sham Tseng.

From Tuen Mun	First bus	5.30 a.m.
	Last bus	11.15 p.m.
From Sham Shui Po	First bus	6.30 a.m.
	Last bus	12.20 p.m.

Bus #53 from Yuen Long East to Castle Peak calls at Tsing Lung Tau and Tsuen Wan:

The MacLehose Trail

From Yuen Long	First bus	5.50 a.m.
	Last bus	11.45 p.m.
From Tsuen Wan	First bus	6.10 a.m.
	Last bus	12.15 p.m.

There are two campsites on the route, the first at the start and the second at Tin Fu Tsai at the very end of the section. There are no places for meals or snacks, so bring food and drink.

*　　*　　*　　*

The forest between Stage 9 and Sek Kong

Section 10
Tin Fu Tsai to Tuen Mun
Difficulty: Grade 1. Time Estimate: 5-6 hours; 15.6 km

Tranquil wooded islands, shooting up from the depths of Tai Lam Chung Reservoir in the heart of Tai Lam Chung Country Park are the the main features of this long but very easy walk.

From the quiet village of Tin Fu Tsai to the reservoir, it's a short walk followed by a very long section along the reservoir's side. Finally, you'll climb to a path alongside a water catchment as you approach the new industrial centre of Tuen Mun.

This is a day's expedition (if you count the transport to/from the city), but the good news is that it's the easiest section on the whole trail: totally flat for most of the way, which is a rarity in Hong Kong. It's a good way to build up some stamina reserves for harder sections if you're relatively inexperienced. The ground can be covered very quickly, in fact I did both Sections Nine and

Flash-flood after a tropical rainstorm at Tai Lam Chung Reservoir

The MacLehose Trail

Ten back-to-back easily, in less than half a day. The latter part near Tuen Mun gives you a good idea of how twentieth century industry has come to an unequal stand-off with Hong Kong's peasant past.

This part is an ideal 'stepping stone' if you want some training before moving onto a harder grade two section. There's also a great way to end the MacLehose Trail and return to Central by using the hover ferry from Tuen Mun pier. It's one of the easiest sections to navigate for anyone who feels hopeless with maps. Most of it is on concrete road and there are very few ambiguous junctions.

Forest next to Section 10

1. ROUTE DETAILS

Tin Fu Tsai to Tai Lam Chung Reservoir

The remote grassy village of Tin Fu Tsai is the start of Section Ten. The road is simply a continuation of Section Nine. Otherwise, access is from the coastal road to the south. The bus stop at Tsing Lung Tau is the best point of approach (see Excursion 4 for complete details), though it's about 8km from here to the start of the trail. After getting off the bus, go past Yuen Tun Camp and head north on a concrete road. There are several paths to Tsing Fai Tong Village to your right; from here pick up the only path north to Tin Fu Tsai, where you'll hit a concrete road. Go left on the trail.

The village of Tin Fu Tsai is spread out beneath the foot of a hill to your right, behind a bamboo screen.

There are joke signs at the entrance of the village to places such as Cambodia and Czechoslovakia! Coming out of the woods by the village, the bare hills behind the reservoir open up in front of you after about fifteen minutes. Despite the village, there was absolutely no traffic on this road on a weekend so you won't be able to hitch should the weather turn bad. It's a 'restricted access' road, even though the road is shown as going to the coast on the map. There are many such roads in the country parks, the restricted access is designed to prevent annoying traffic and preserve the peacefulness of the area.

After another 15-minute downhill walk, you'll find a picnic area and emergency telephone at the head of the reservoir. Fol-

An autumn day in Tai Lam Chung Country Park

low signs taking you left after a bridge and right at the next immediate split. If you want an escape route, follow the signs for Castle Peak Road. In another ten minutes, the trail splits left at a beautiful picnic site by the reservoir, and down a path. Straightaway the path goes left at a fork and sticks close to the shore of the reservoir until it meets the road again in about 7km (or at least an hour's easy flat walk).

The trail near Tuen Mun

This section was completely deserted when I walked it and the whole expanse of the lake was utterly still, with the islands rising in the middle. At the finish of the path you join the main road after a small rise, and go left on the concrete road.

Past the small, grassy dam, go right at a split next to the emergency telephone and join the water catchment. You'll follow this for a good 7 or 8 km almost to the end of the trail. Shortly the high-rises of Tuen Mun come into view in the distance, so you know you're within striking distance of the finish of the trail. The approach runs about 2 kms. above and parallel to the Tuen Mun Road, going past the extended village of So Kwun Wat Tsuen on the left. Keep following this water catchment past the con-

The MacLehose Trail

tainer storage area in the valley on your left. You will notice shortly a recreational zone on the left that features a fitness trail with many exercises to suit different tastes. Ignore the smaller paths to the left including one that says 'Welcome to Tuen Mun New Town'. You will eventually see a flat grassy plateau, which is a water service station. You'll arrive at it just after going past stage one of the fitness trail. There is a major signpost directing you down some steps at the back of this construction.

This small path descends for ten minutes through a few ramshackle houses with banana trees before you come to the rather unspectacular official end to the trail under a flyover at the junction of Castle Peak and Pui To Road. Before joining the ratrace again, why not have a meal or a few refreshments. The taxi-ride to the ferry costs about $20 from here.

2. FEATURES OF THE ROUTE

Tai Lam Chung Reservoir has a vast and tranquil feel to it, but the last section of the route towards Tuen Mun is of most interest for the obvious and grating clash it presents between the old and the new. Whilst farmers potter about in carefully culti-

Another look at the main reservoir on a rainy day

The MacLehose Trail

Tuen Mun and Reservoir

vated paddy fields, lorries on their way to the container port have their crashing rhythm of work. It presents a surreal and unexpected scene after the grandeur of much of the rest of the trail. Clearly the most valuable crop here is the land itself, with farmers renting it out to store containers, or even selling it off (and becoming rich overnight) so that the site of much of their previous toil can be covered in a concrete blanket.

Further towards Tuen Mun the beaches come into view, dwarfed by the skyscrapers, and Castle Peak rises in the background with the steep trail climbing its side and radio masts on top. Castle Peak is home to the Castle Peak Monastery, established more than 1,500 years ago. Castle Peak Bay, which is the first bay you see before turning the corner of the water catchment to head north, was once a calling point for boats from the Indian Ocean and the Middle East, who waited there for the monsoon winds to carry them to Canton. Now it is a popular swimming beach, although pollution has become a problem in recent years!

Modern day Tuen Mun is a product of a dramatic 1970's housing programme by the government, aimed at reducing the acute problem of squatters within the territory. Like Shatin and Tsuen Wan it was built 'as a whole' with complete facilities and excel-

The MacLehose Trail

lent transport links for those to be housed there. But unlike the former two towns, Tuen Mun has suffered a number of social problems, many related to triads and youth gangs.

3. TRANSPORT AND OTHER DETAILS

After getting to the ferry by taxi, skim over the waves back to Central and get a good look at the western side of the New Territories coast and Kowloon.

Times of Tuen Mun - Hong Kong Hover Ferry:

Tuen Mun - Central

First and last Hover Ferry

Monday to Friday:	6.30 am. and 7.40 pm.
Sunday:	6.55 am. and 7.40 pm.

* * * *

Graves near Yuen Tun (page 131)

The MacLehose Trail

Excursion 4
Tsing Lung Tau to Sham Tseng

The walk from Tsing Lung Tau to Sham Tseng via Tai Lam Chung Country Park is about 7km. It can be walked comfortably within four hours. Degree of difficulty is a 2 and a 3 when it has been raining. Give yourself a full day to really enjoy it, especially if you want to have dinner at leisure afterwards in Sham Tseng.

Even the most enthusiastic hikers of my acquaintance tend to be ignorant of the fact that there is a lot of countryside still to be discovered between the traditional MacLehose Trail and the shoreline that runs between Tsuen Wan and Tuen Mun. I had made a few forays over the years, but was alerted only last year about this hike by my friend Alan Crawley, long-time resident of Hong Kong and an indomitable hiker himself.

To get to the starting point of this excursion, take the MTR to Tsuen Wan (final stop) and walk to the western exit. The bus

Lush vegetation in the June sun

The MacLehose Trail

Looking east towards Tsuen Wan

station is located below Nan Fung Centre and can be seen just across the road. However, to get the right public transport, you need to walk over the pedestrian flyover one road further south. Castle Peak Road continues here west.

You should position yourself between the Hong Kong Bank branch on the corner and the Telecom CSL shop (100m down the road) to catch KMB bus 52X (HK$4.30 to Tuen Mun Town Centre) or minibus 96 or 96M to Tsing Lung Tau. The latter is actually your best bet, as it runs every five mins and stops on the exact access road you need to take for this hike into the hills.

Once you pass Sham Tseng (your final destination for the hike) which is the home of Hong Kong's premier beer San Miguel and the countless goose restaurants, it is time to make sure you get off at the right point (if you travel on 52X). There are a number of newly built high-rises by Hong Kong's largest developer Sun Hung Kai on this stretch of Castle Peak Road.

Tsing Lung Tau is just around the corner of the last one called 'Sea Crest Villa'. This new town has an unimpeded view of the new bridge between Tsing Yi, Ma Wan and Lantau Islands (see

The MacLehose Trail

Construction of the suspension bridge: Ma Wan - Lantau

photo of the beach). There is a lovely Taoist temple just 200m from Lung Yue Road where PLB 96 turns right.

There are several soft drink stores on the corner that allow you to provision yourself. The road begins a steady ascent and passes under the Tuen Mun highway. One of the most common mistakes made by hikers (including myself in the past) who want to travel along the coast is to get on any bus that leaves from Tsuen Wan west. Most of them take the highway, and you cannot get off until you are in Tuen Mun. This turns out to be a very nice practical joke if you get stuck in a traffic jam. By the time you are in Tuen Mun, there may not be enough time to do your planned walk!

It is almost exactly 1km from the beach to the start of the country park where there is a fork in the secondary road. The road stops rising at this point if you take the road to the Country Park Management Centre (straight ahead). You will find a map of the countryside on the left. We are taking the road to the left towards Yuen Tun. There is a barrier across the road normally manned during day-light hours by a warden. This road swivels left and continues to climb steadily. The bridge to Lantau and the new airport can be seen even more clearly once you round the corner. The split in the road to Yuen Tun (Civil Aid Services Camp) occurs after about 1,200m. Please continue in the direction of Tsing Fai Tong. You will hear a brook running on the right.

After about 150m, i.e. once you round the next corner, you will find a bridge over a shallow pool of water. Just across it on the left you will see a path that leads uphill through the bushes. If you have no intention of going on this excursion but just want to join the 10th section of the MacLehose Trail, please continue straight ahead along the hardened secondary road. The Country Park Management Centre on the most north-eastern spot of Tai Lam Chung Reservoir will be reached within an hour from this point by following (1) on the map in the back of this book.

The main adventure of our excursion (trail 2) actually starts here. The path is surprisingly good through the bushes, the main reason being that there are a lot of graves on the slope, many of them recently dug and well-

Temple on Castle Peak Road (page 130)

The MacLehose Trail

tended (see photo on page 127). Follow the red pieces of cloths when in doubt. They have been hung there by 'orienteering' squads or the local chapter of Hash House Harriers (internationally redoubted explorers of the countryside). Once you reach the highest point, there are three paths you can take. Opt for the middle one that will give you the easiest access through the forest to the other side of the hill. The path occasionally becomes very vague but by following the red ribbons and keeping to the crest, you eventually will descend to the trail that runs diametrically across and connects Yuen Tun with the MacLehose Trail. There is here an unimpeded view of Tai Lam Chung Reservoir and Tuen Mun to the west (see photo on page 126).

Turn right at this trail. The descent is rather steep for comfort during rainy weather (about 30m in height). You will shortly come to a brook. It becomes a rough but regular path through the bushes further on: at least twice as broad as the trail over the hill you just took. You will see a marker on the right that indicates that Sek Kong is straight ahead. Take the path uphill to the right pointing (again) towards Tsing Fai Tong (5.6km.). You will shortly reach

Tsing Fai Tong hamlet (page 134)

The MacLehose Trail

Tai Lam Chung during the wet monsoon

the main secondary road where a left turn would take you to the MacLehose Trail (Tai Lam Chung Reservoir 1.4km) and a right turn back to Tsing Lung Tau (now a distant 4.8km). Cross instead to continue on the contour walk on the other side indicated on the marker by Tsing Fai Tong. The distance has even increased. The reason is that you will be walking the contours of the hills instead of the more direct secondary road.

The next stretch is even easier to follow although I have never met a soul on four walks so far. The trail zig-zags around the hills and rises and descends elegantly. There is a beautiful grave towards the end of the trail (before you get off) on the right, after which you come to another marker with four directions. Take the one to the right towards Tsing Lung Tau; the Country Parks Warden Post is about 50m up. You may have become disoriented by turning so frequently in all directions. To get your bearings right, study the main map (Sheet 6 of Series HM20C). The secondary road to the right (to Tai Lam Chung) leads back to where you were 15 mins ago, and the road on the left to Tin Fu Tsai Camp

The MacLehose Trail

(close to the MacLehose Trail). Our excursion continues instead across the road back towards to Tsing Lung Tau and Tsing Fai Tong. The path to the latter hamlet will be found shortly on the left.

The going on this new trail is good. After about 1km you will cross a brook where you could even have a swim. The water tends to be cool on a hot day. There is another crossroads just up the hill from here, your last chance to go to Tai Lam Chung (on the left) and Tsing Lung Tau (on the right). Stay on the straight and narrow which will lead you to a concrete path that connects Sham Tseng and Tsing Fai Tong. This hamlet lies just a minute's walk to the north and is inhabited by less than a dozen people and as many dogs and cows.

The valley stretching to Tsing Lung Tau has in the meantime appeared on the right. To reach Sham Tseng, you must follow the concrete path away from Tsing Fai Tong towards the sea. The path turns slowly left to another valley from where it descends towards Sham Tseng. A lot of changes will take place in the next two years. The main high-way (Route 3) to Yuen Long will be built through the country park using a tunnel which will start at the planned bridge-crossing from Ma Wan and Tsing Yi to Ting Kau (between Sham Tseng and Tsuen Wan).

The concrete path ends near the Tuen Mun highway, and then descends under it. Where it meets the main village road, turn left. The first restaurant on the right called 'Yue Kee' and its cousin 'Nang Kee' started the craze for roasted goose in Hong Kong. Even governors have lunched and dined here. The food is indeed excellent and the prices still reasonable. Castle Peak Road is 200m onwards from where public transport (PLB 96) will whisk you back to Tsuen Wan within 20 mins. A lovely outing!

*   *   *   *

The MacLehose Trail

APPENDICES
A. Route Profiles
B. Route Maps
C. Excursions

A. Route Profiles

(Elevation above MSL)
Graded from I to III
according to degree of difficulty

The MacLehose Trail

SECTION 1 - GRADE I

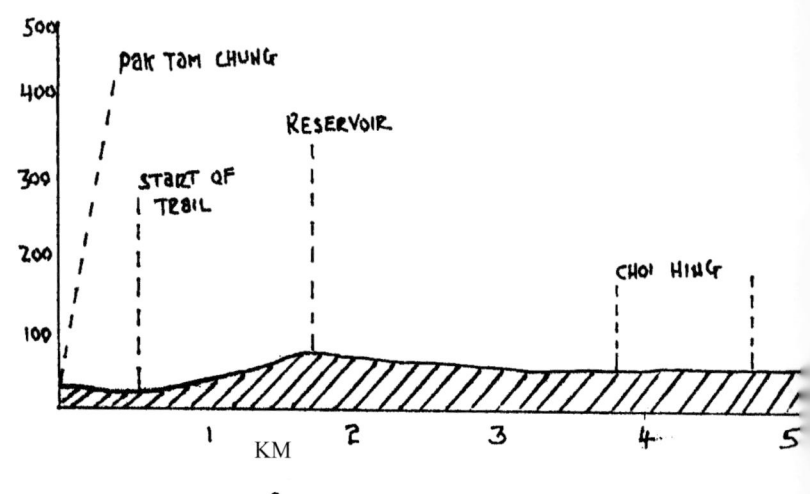

ALTITUDE ~ METRES.

pak tom chung / start of trail / reservoir / choi hung

KILOMETRES.

SECTION 2 - GRADE II

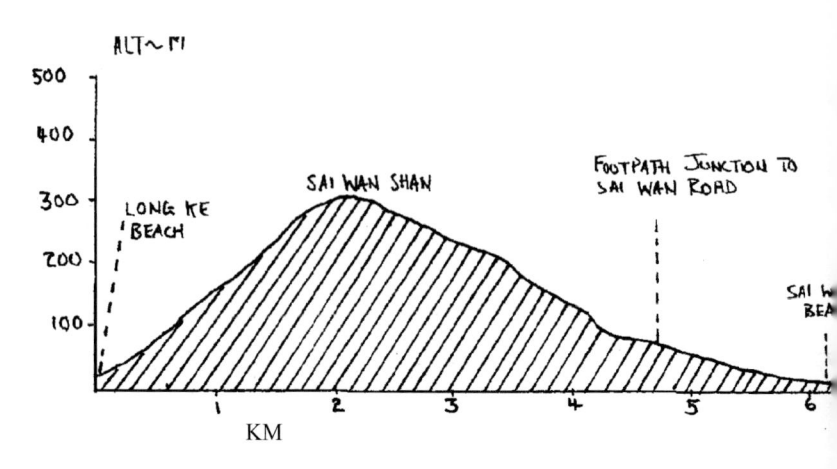

ALT ~ M

LONG KE BEACH / SAI WAN SHAN / FOOTPATH JUNCTION TO SAI WAN ROAD / SAI WAN BEACH

KM

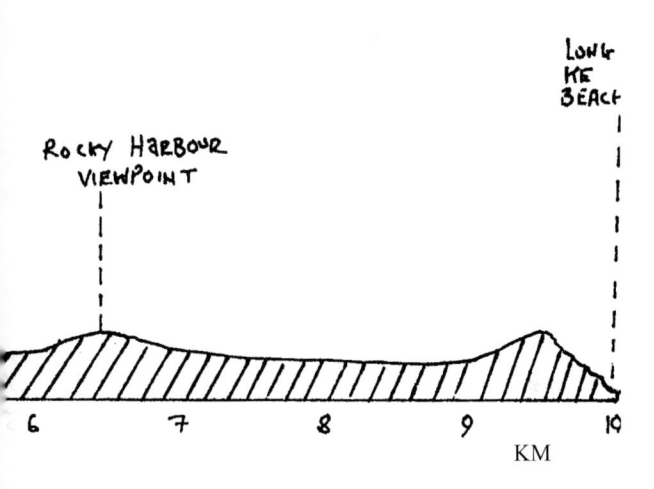

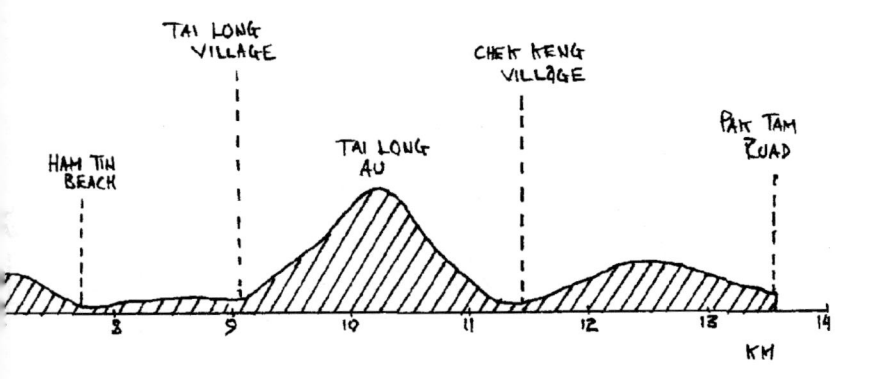

The MacLehose Trail

The MacLehose Trail

SECTION 3 - GRADE III

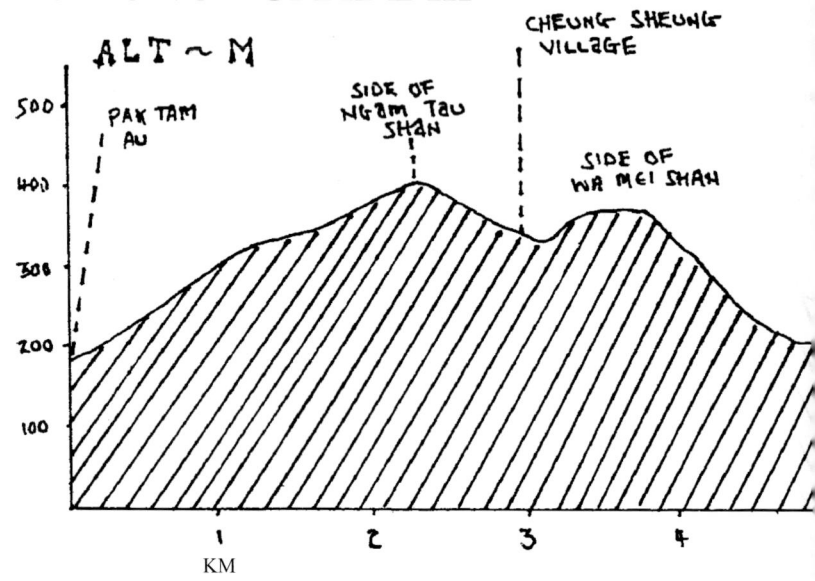

Elevation profile (ALT ~ M) showing: Pak Tam Au (start), Side of Ngam Tau Shan (~420m at ~2.3km), Cheung Sheung Village (~3km), Side of Wa Mei Shan (~400m at ~4km).

SECTION 4 - GRADE III

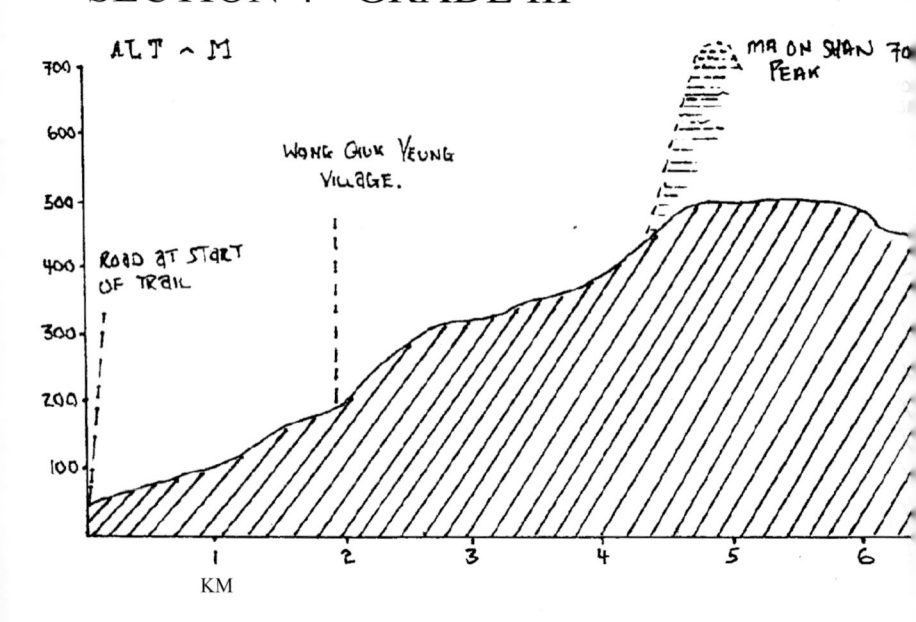

Elevation profile (ALT ~ M) showing: Road at start of trail (~0km), Wong Chuk Yeung Village (~2km, ~200m), rising to ~500m by 4.5km, with Ma On Shan Peak (~700m) at ~5km.

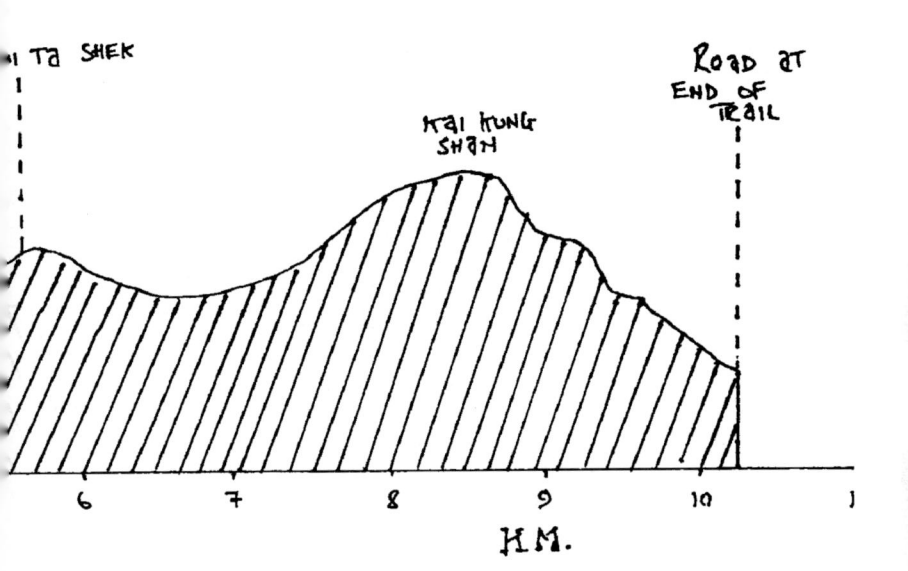

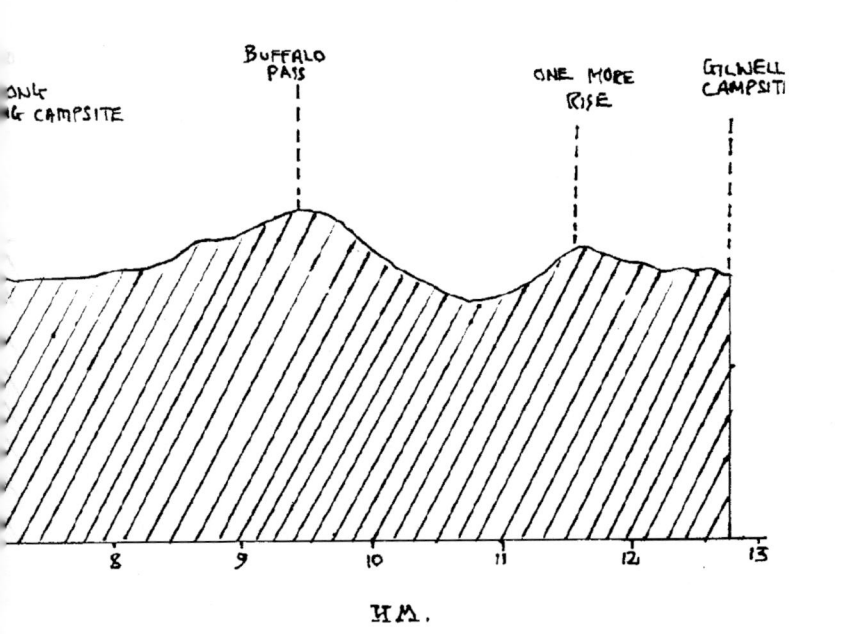

The MacLehose Trail

SECTION 5 - GRADE II

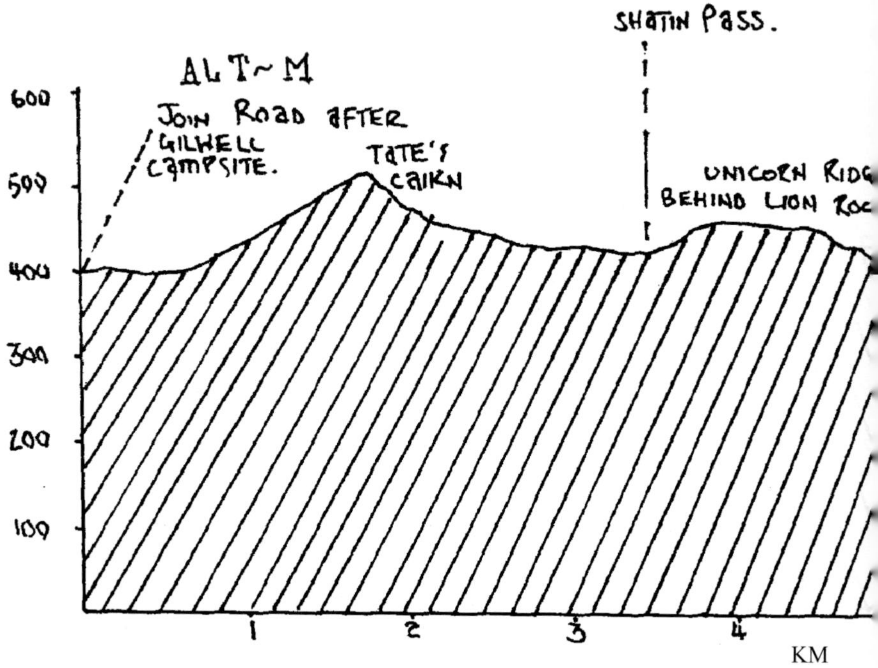

SHATIN PASS.
ALT~M
600
500
400
300
200
100
JOIN ROAD AFTER GILWELL CAMPSITE.
TATE'S CAIRN
UNICORN RIDG
BEHIND LION ROC
1
2
3
4
KM

SECTION 6 - GRADE I

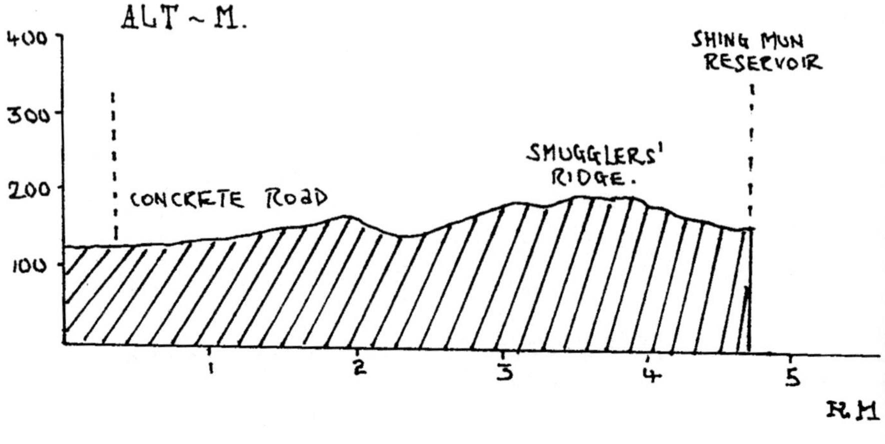

ALT ~ M.
400
300
200
100
SHING MUN RESERVOIR
SMUGGLERS' RIDGE.
CONCRETE ROAD
1
2
3
4
5
R.M

The MacLehose Trail

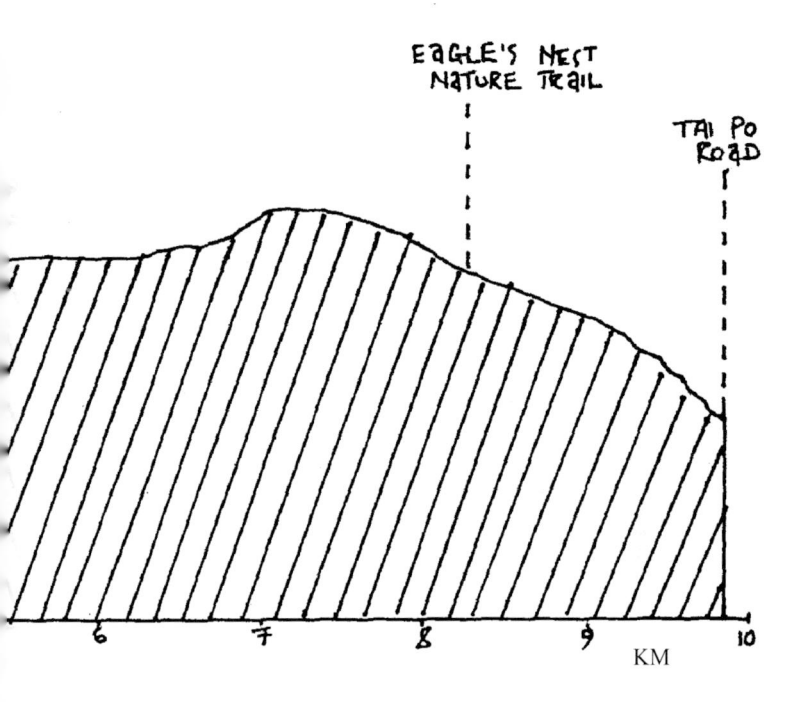

Profile of Lion Rock and Beacon Hill seen from Kam Shan

The MacLehose Trail

SECTION 7 - GRADE II

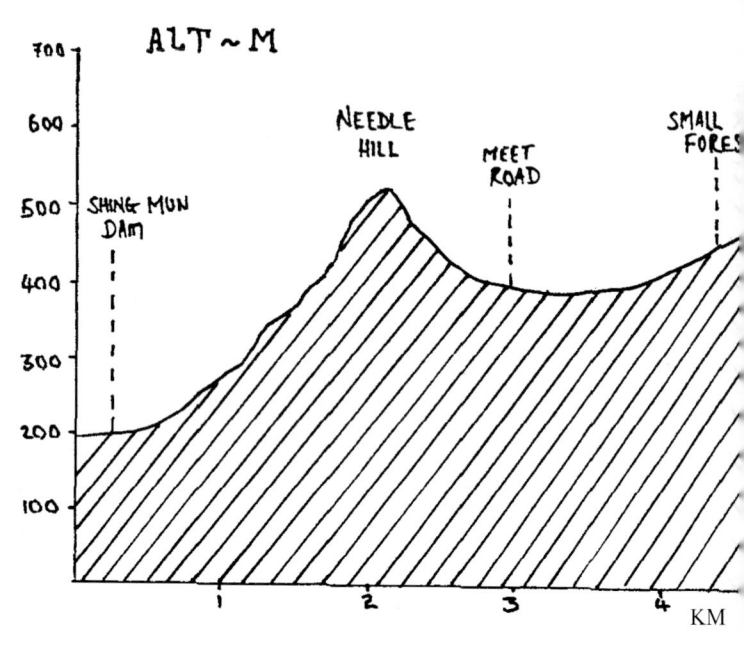

ALT ~ M

- SHING MUN DAM
- NEEDLE HILL
- MEET ROAD
- SMALL FOREST

KM

Near Cove Hill

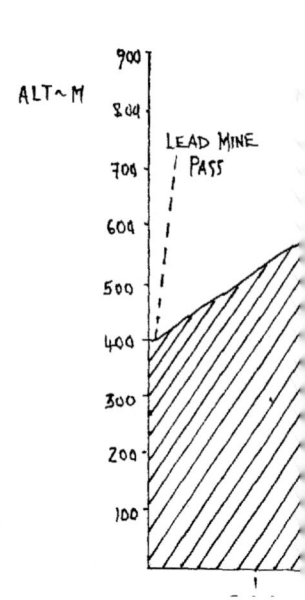

ALT ~ M

- LEAD MINE PASS

The MacLehose Trail

Tai To Yan and Sek Kong valley (near Tai Mo Shan)

SECTION 8 - GRADE II

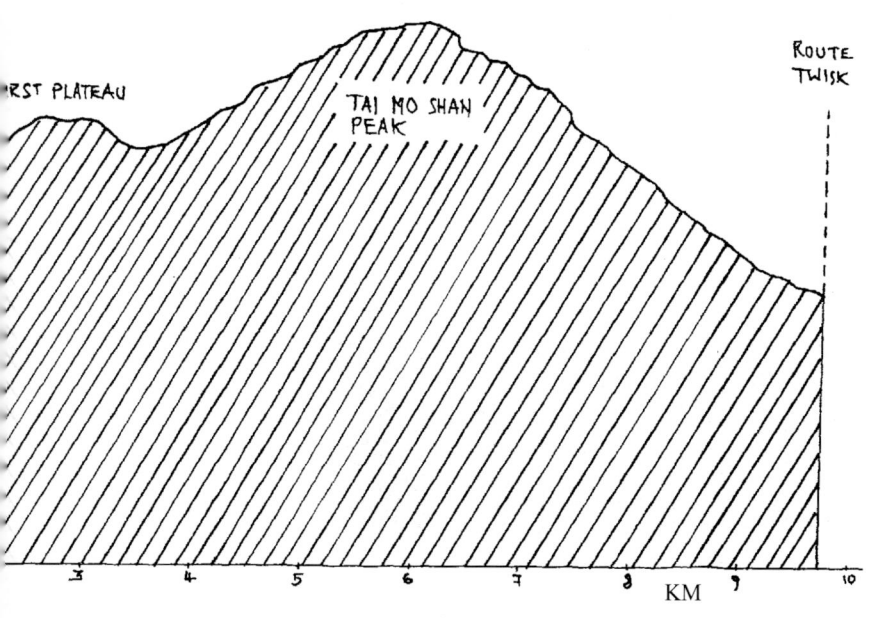

SECTION 9 - GRADE I

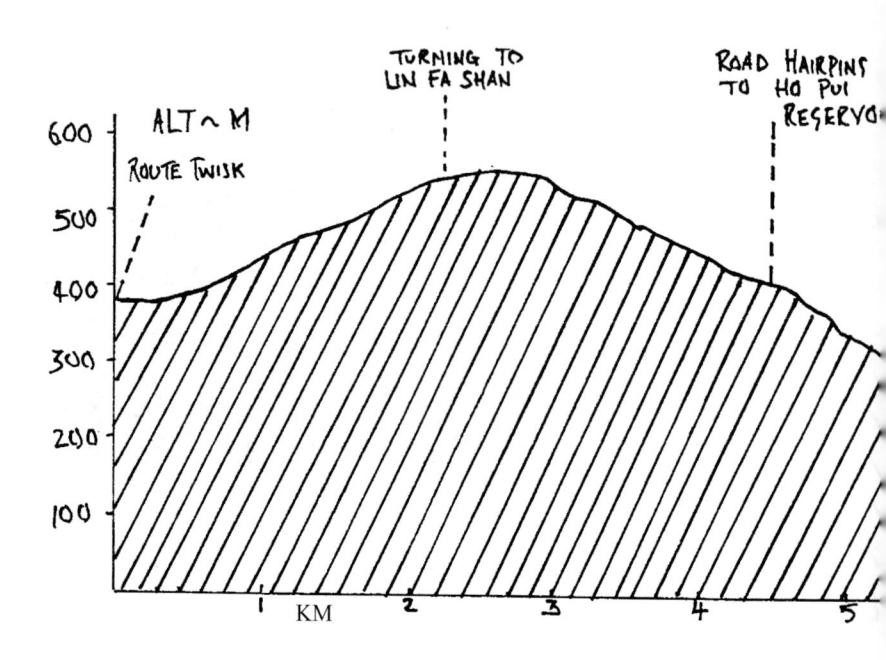

SECTION 10 - GRADE I

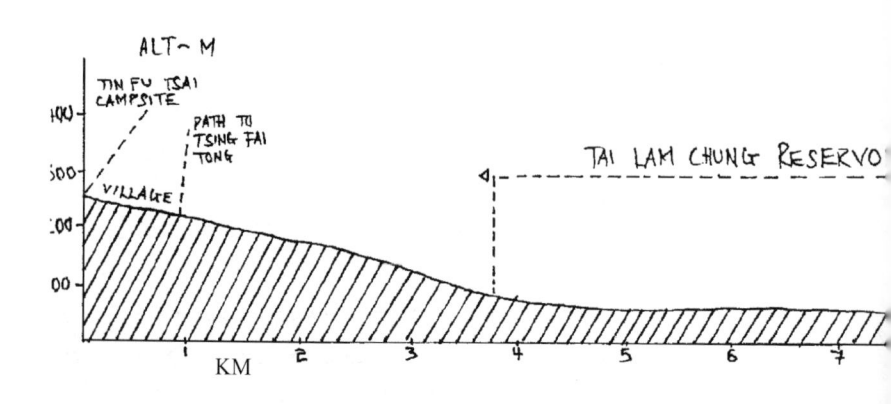

The MacLehose Trail

*North Lantau's changing appearance
(seen from Castle Peak Road)*

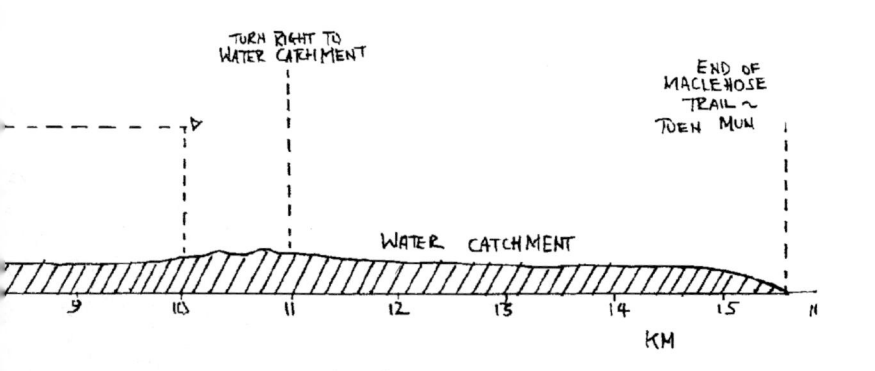

The MacLehose Trail

Two more views of Section 3

The MacLehose Trail

B. Route Maps

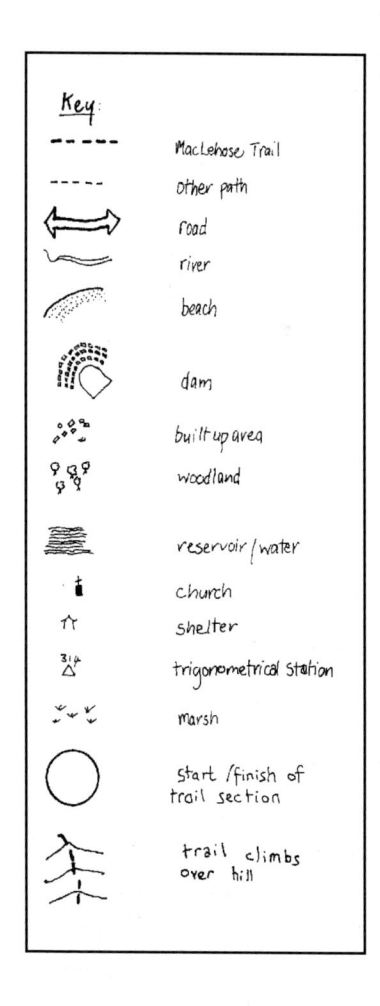

Key:

– – – –	MacLehose Trail
- - - -	other path
⟷	road
~~	river
	beach
	dam
	built up area
	woodland
	reservoir / water
	church
⌂	shelter
△ 314	trigonometrical station
	marsh
○	start / finish of trail section
	trail climbs over hill

The MacLehose Trail

Introduction to the Route Maps

"This book is a real guide to the Trail," writes Lord MacLehose in the Foreword to this book. The author and publisher could hope for no better endorsement of their product, or greater appreciation of their humble efforts.

To live up to the user's every expectation, and indeed to ensure the completeness of the book, it was deemed essential that maps be provided as an integral part of the book. To meet this requirement, we had the choice of either including loose sheets of adequately sized maps folded into a wallet within the cover, or to sectionalise the maps to fit the pages of the book. This latter method had the decided advantage that the maps would not be lost or misplaced and the user would have access to them for as long as the book remained in his possession.

Owing to page size, which had to be kept down for convenience of carrying the book around, maps had to be sectionalised — progressing from page to page, or spread page to spread page, as appropriate. In the process of turning to and fro, between successive pages for map reference, some patience and care is called for. The user will, however, soon get used to referring to the maps and have no difficulty in picking out the information he/she needs.

Should you prefer to view the whole map to assist you in getting things in perspective, it is always possible to zerox the map sections before setting out, and scotch tape the separate parts to make up the whole.

The MacLehose Trail generally flows in a westerly direction (i.e. from east to west, or from the right hand side of the page towards the left). Looking at maps on facing pages, you will find that you in fact start on the right page and then come on to the left page — opposite to conventional page flow which is from left to right! Get oriented to geographical direction rather than conventional page flow and you will have no problem with this.

The MacLehose Trail

On the mountain trail

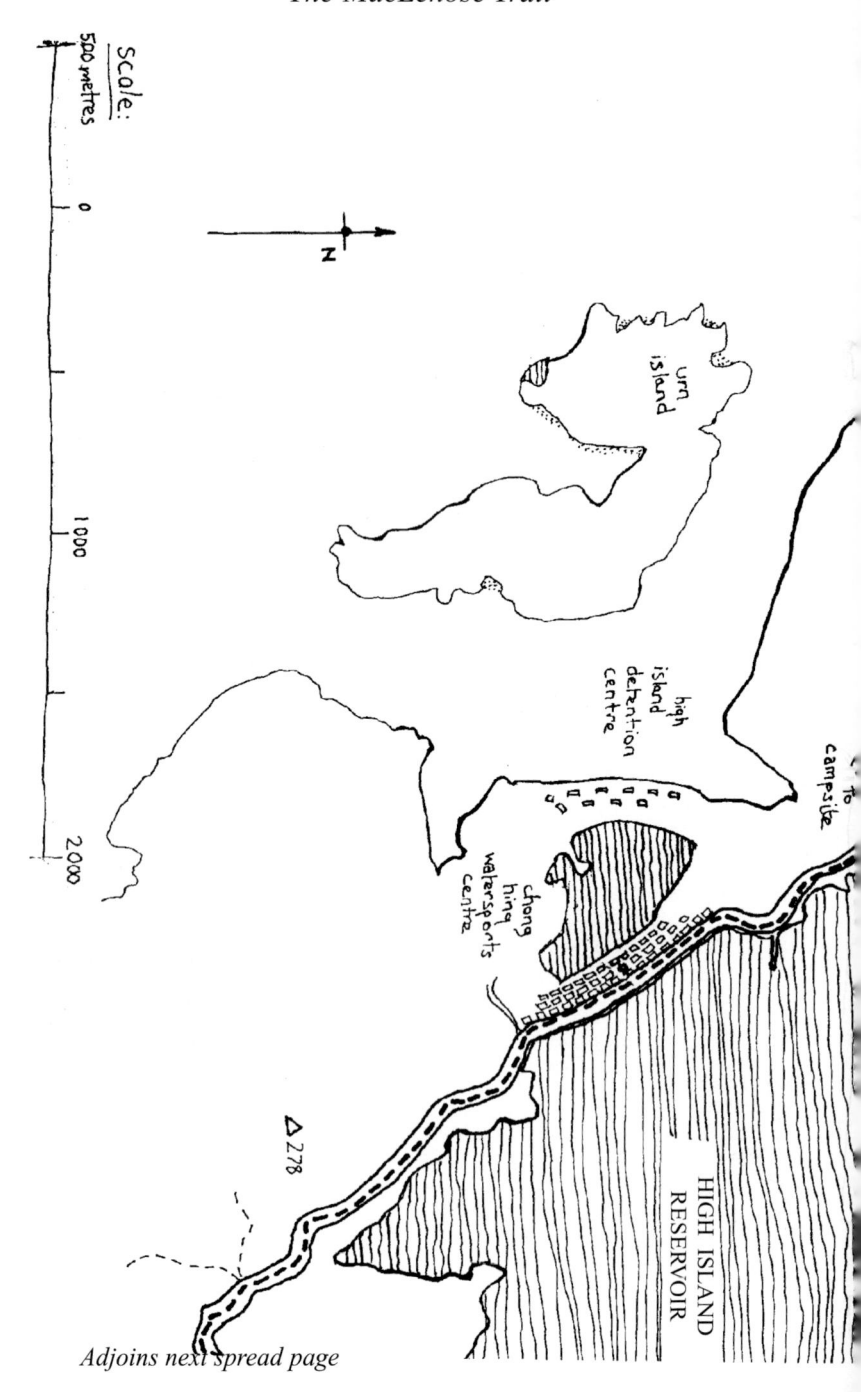

The MacLehose Trail

Adjoins next spread page

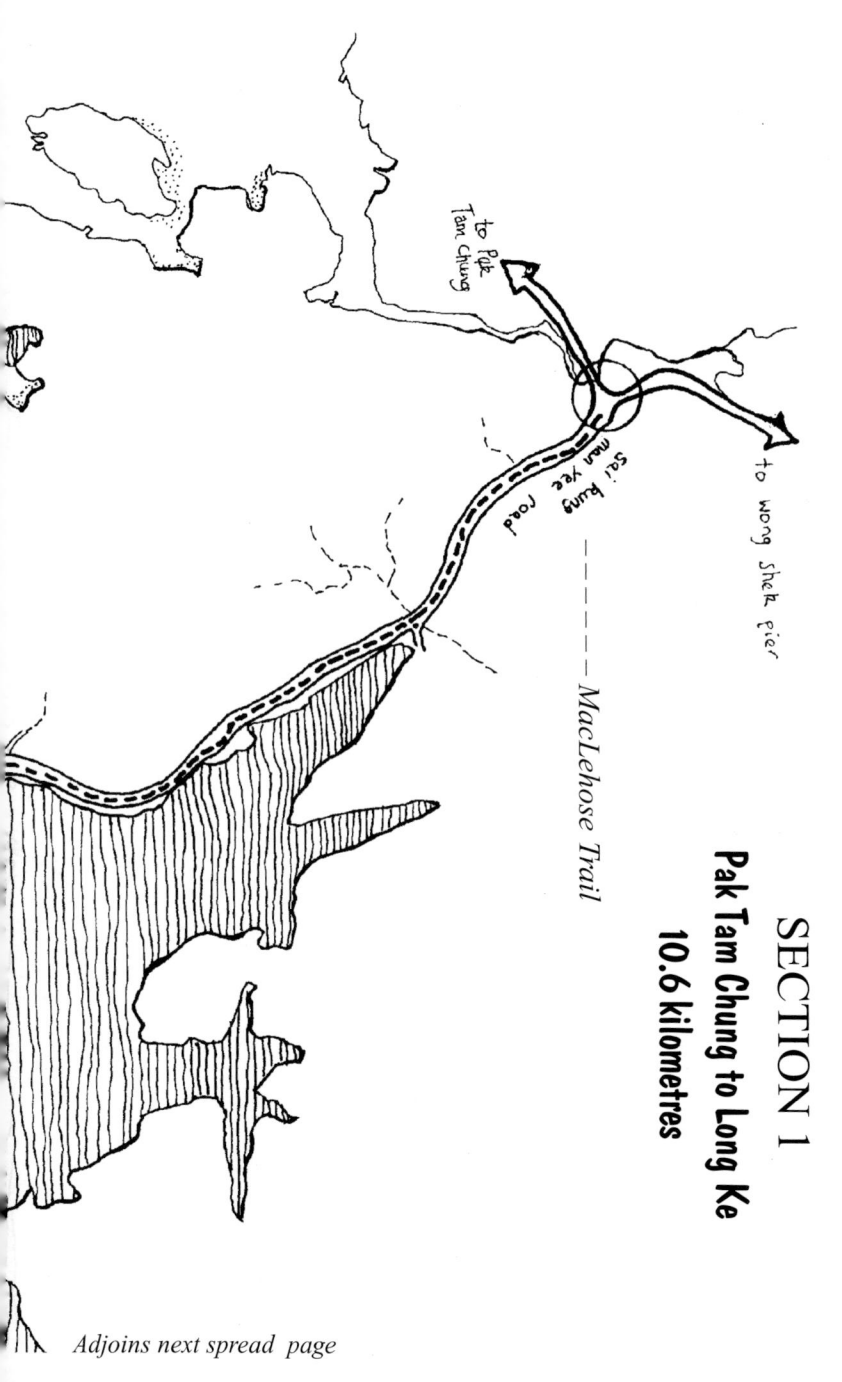

The MacLehose Trail

SECTION 1
Pak Tam Chung to Long Ke
10.6 kilometres

to Pak Tam Chung

to Wong Shek pier

Sai Kung Man Yee road

MacLehose Trail

Adjoins next spread page

The MacLehose Trail

Adjoins previous spread page

HIGH ISLAND RESERVOIR

eastern dam

long Ke beach

monastery

The MacLehose Trail

Adjoins previous spread page

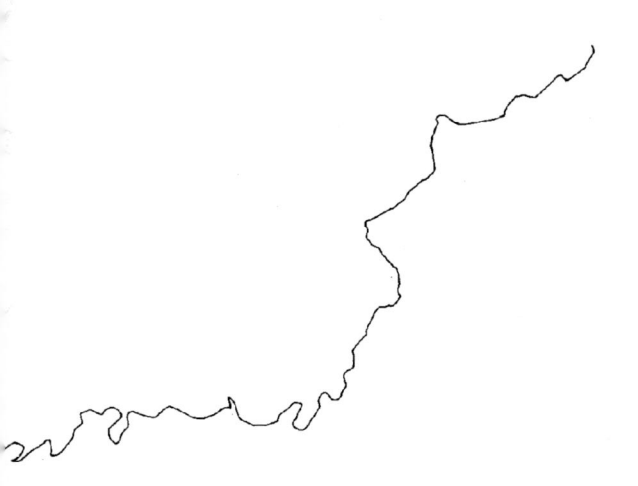

**SECTION 1 (cont'd)
Pak Tam Chung to Long Ke**

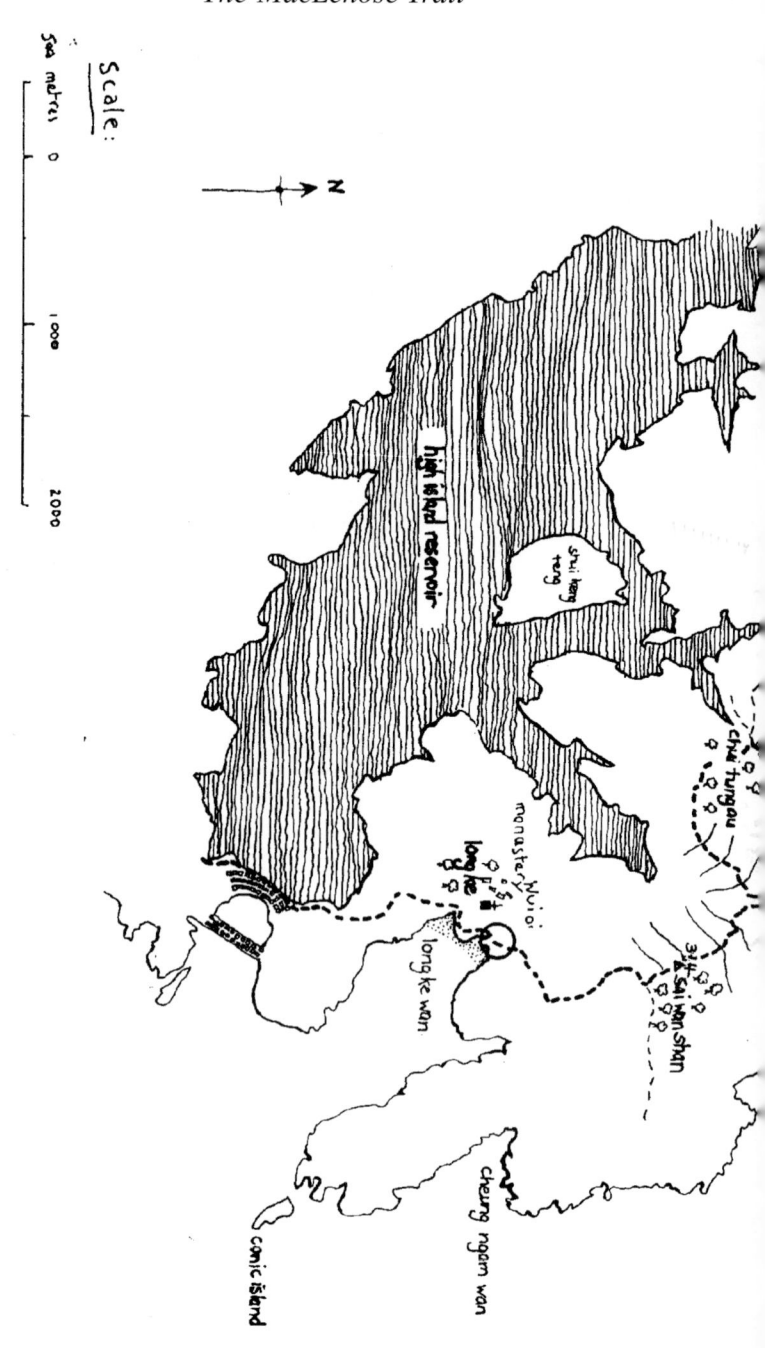

The MacLehose Trail

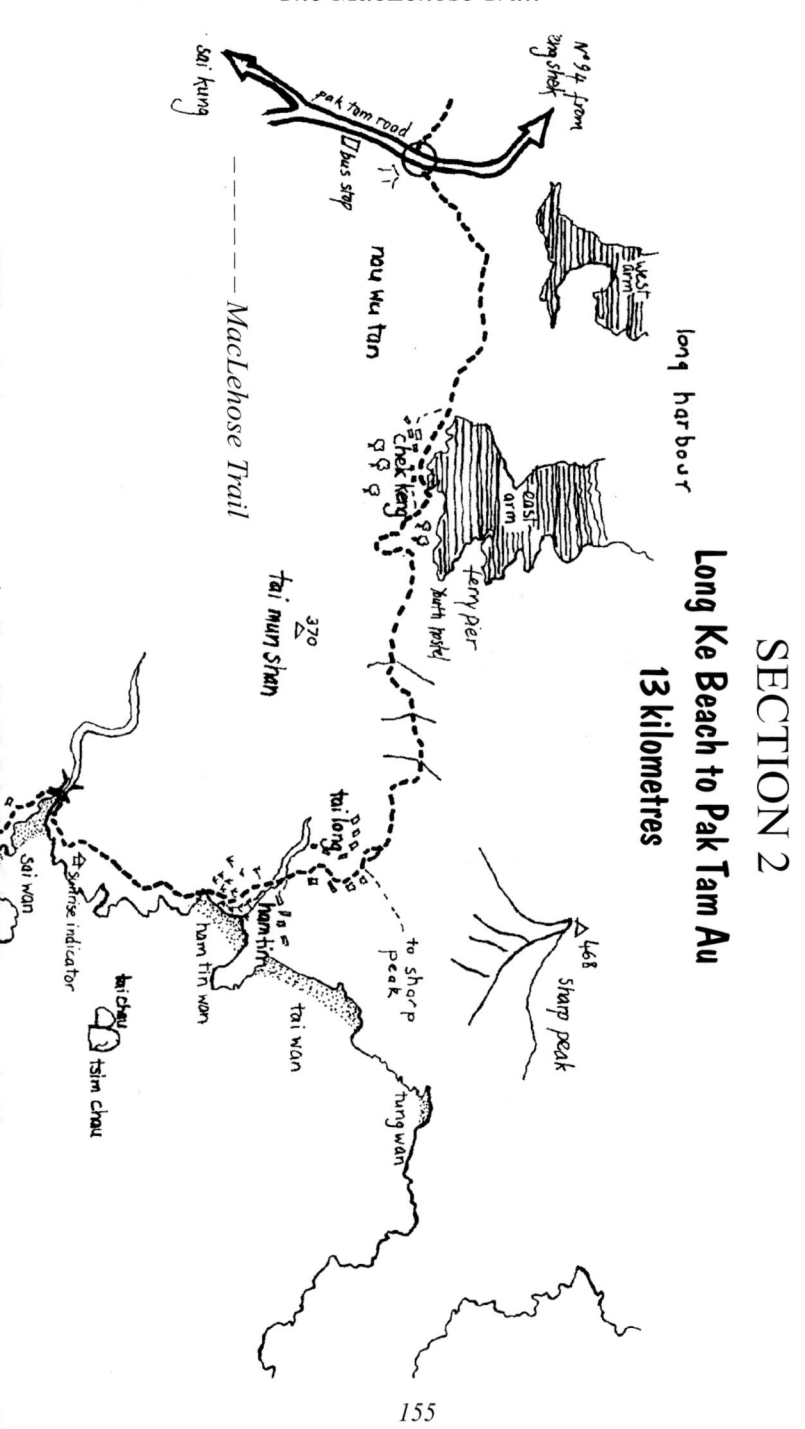

The MacLehose Trail

SECTION 2
Long Ke Beach to Pak Tam Au
13 kilometres

The MacLehose Trail

Adjoins next spread page

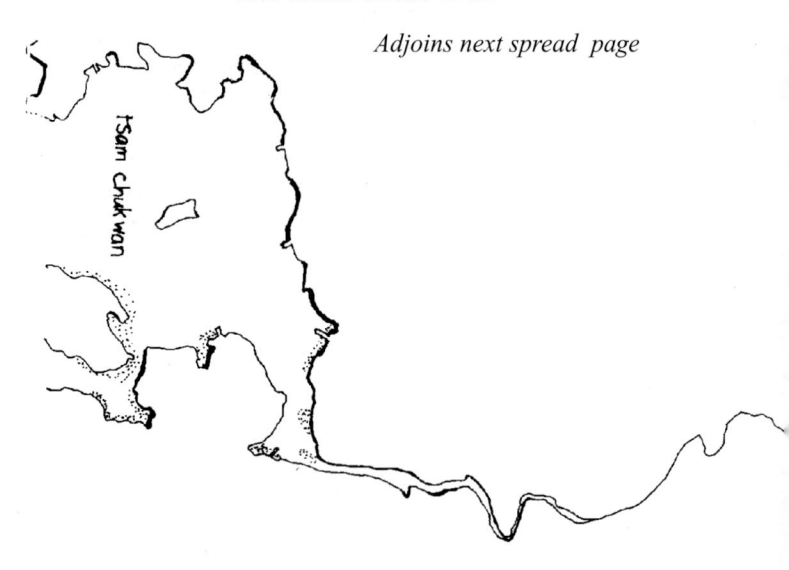

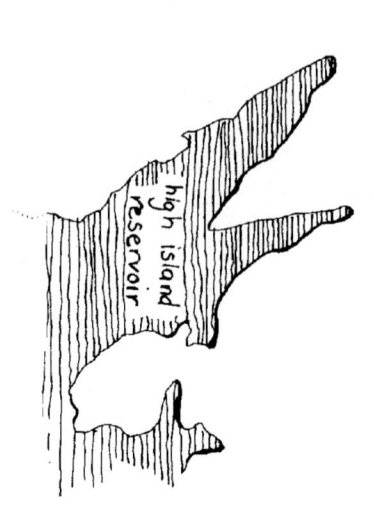

Tsam Chuk wan

high island reservoir

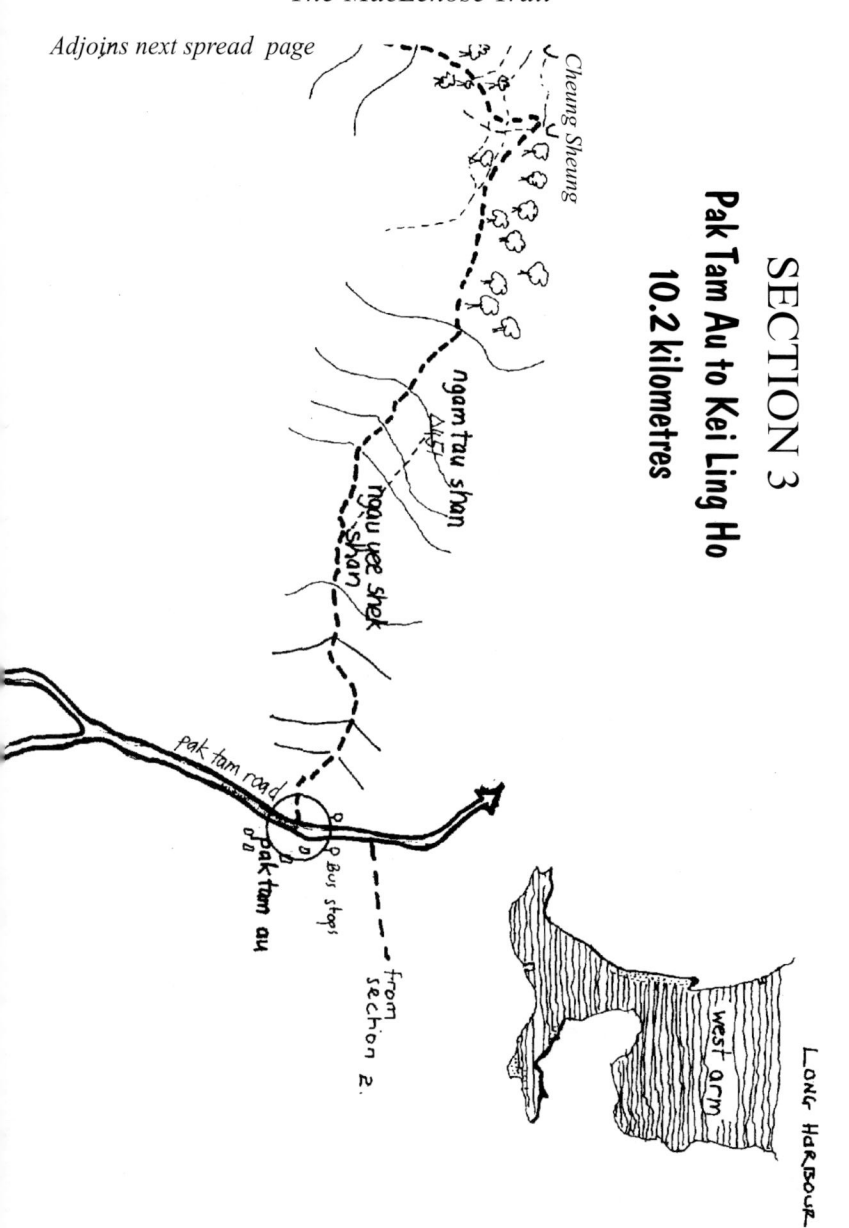

The MacLehose Trail

Adjoins next spread page

SECTION 3
Pak Tam Au to Kei Ling Ho
10.2 kilometres

Cheung Sheung

ngam tau shan

ngau yee shek shan

pak tam road

pak tam au

Bus stops

from section 2.

WEST ARM

LONG HARBOUR

The MacLehose Trail

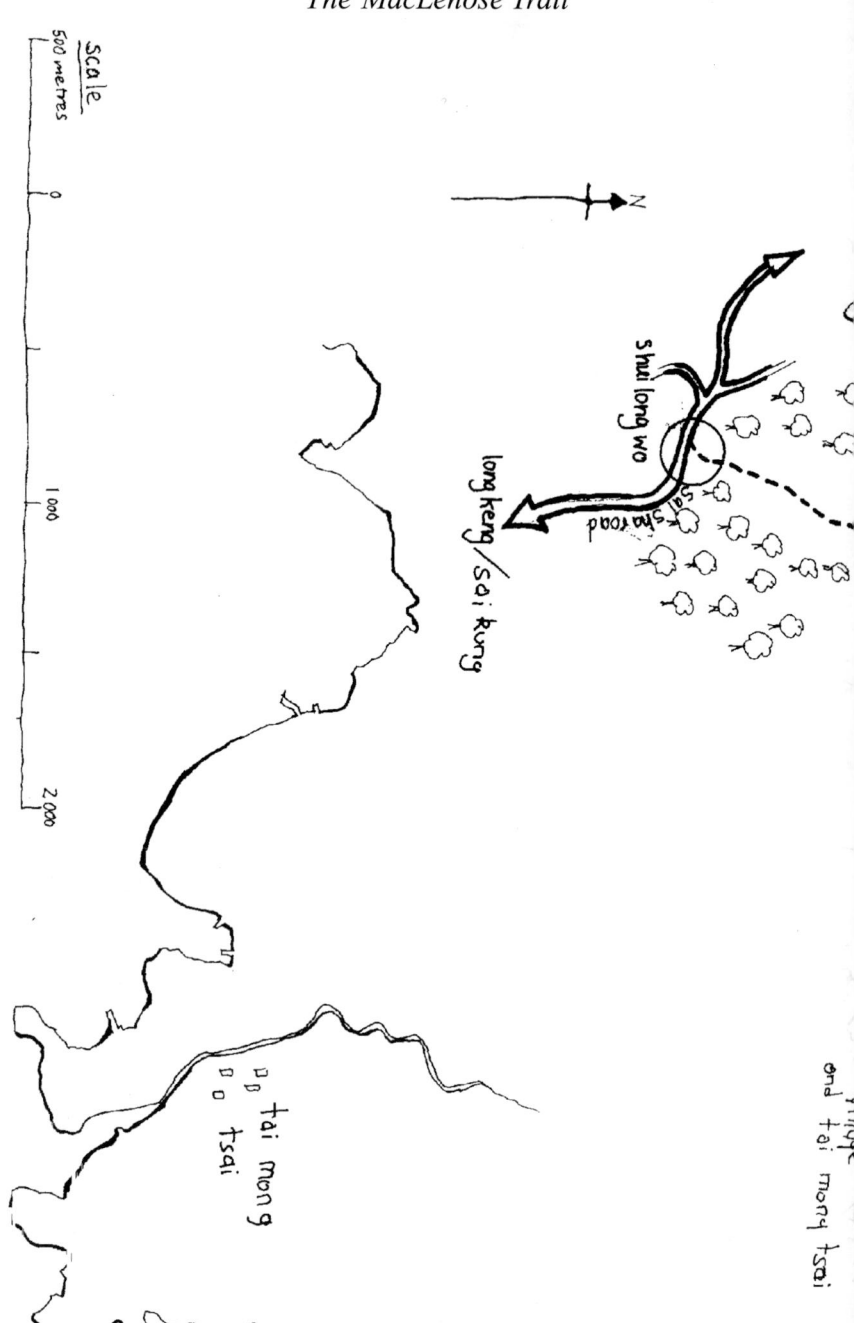

Adjoins previous spread page

The MacLehose Trail

SECTION 3 (Cont'd)
Pak Tam Au to Kei Ling Ho

three fathoms cove

kai kung shan

yung shue O village

Wa Mei Shan

379

------ MacLehose Trail

Adjoins previous spread page

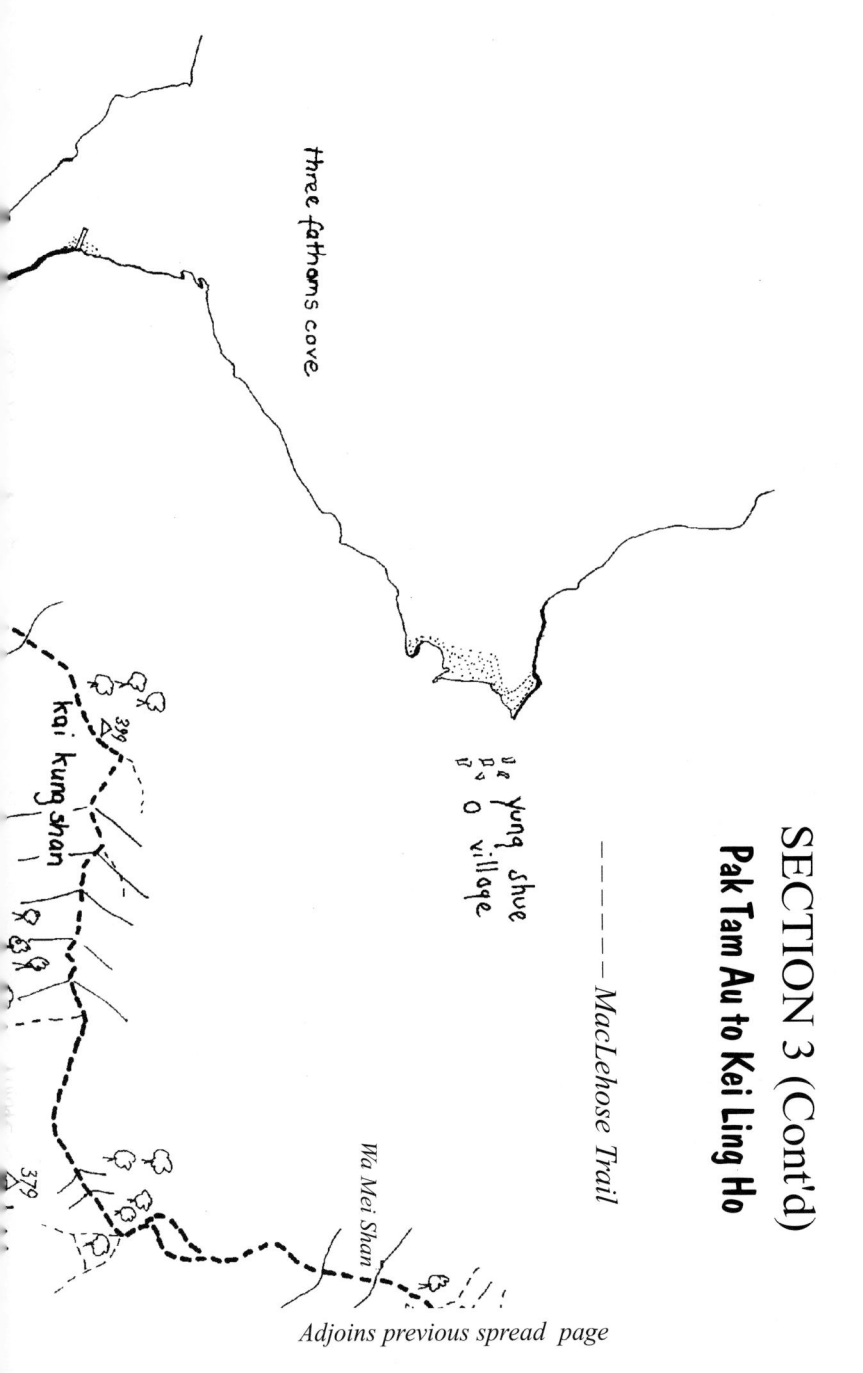

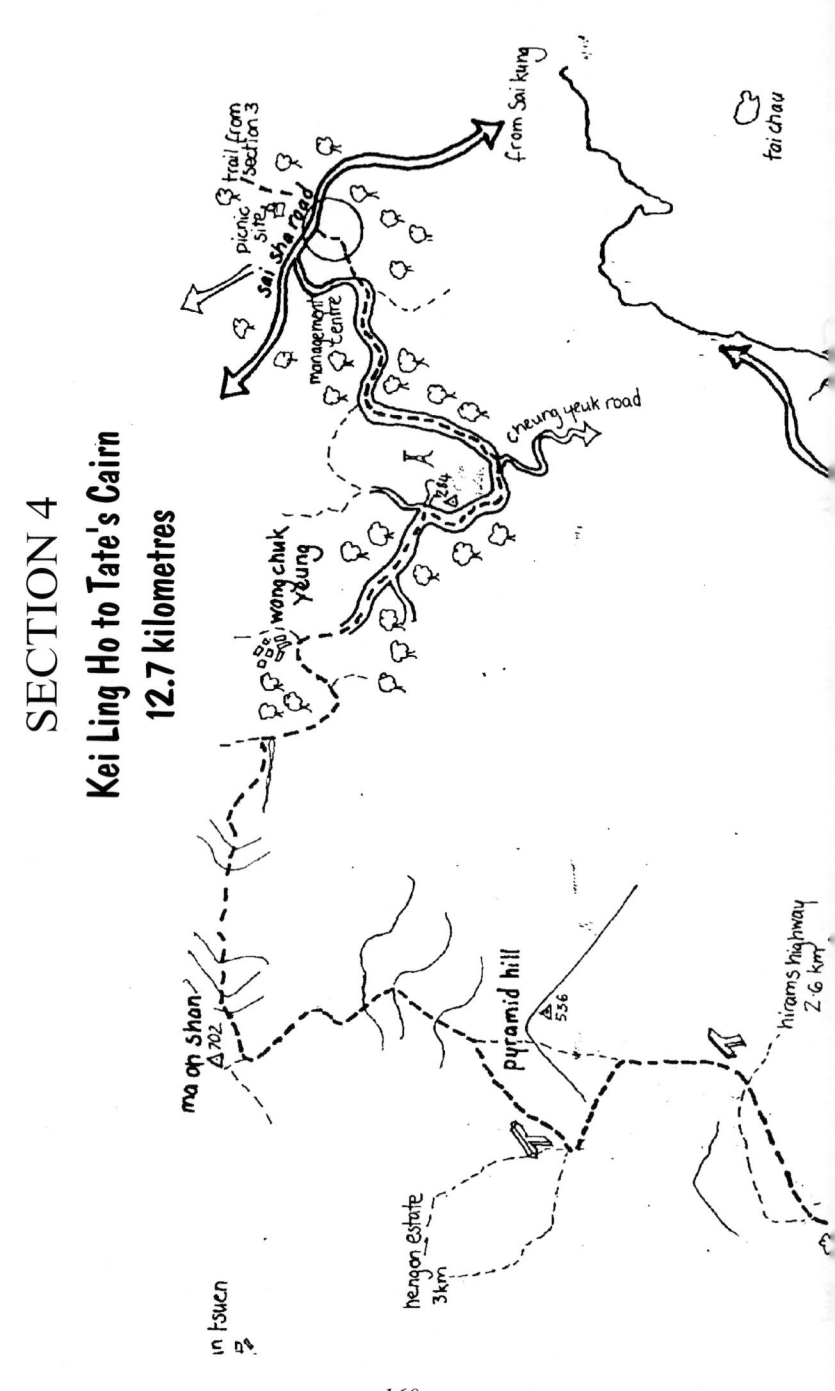

The MacLehose Trail

SECTION 4
Kei Ling Ho to Tate's Cairn
12.7 kilometres

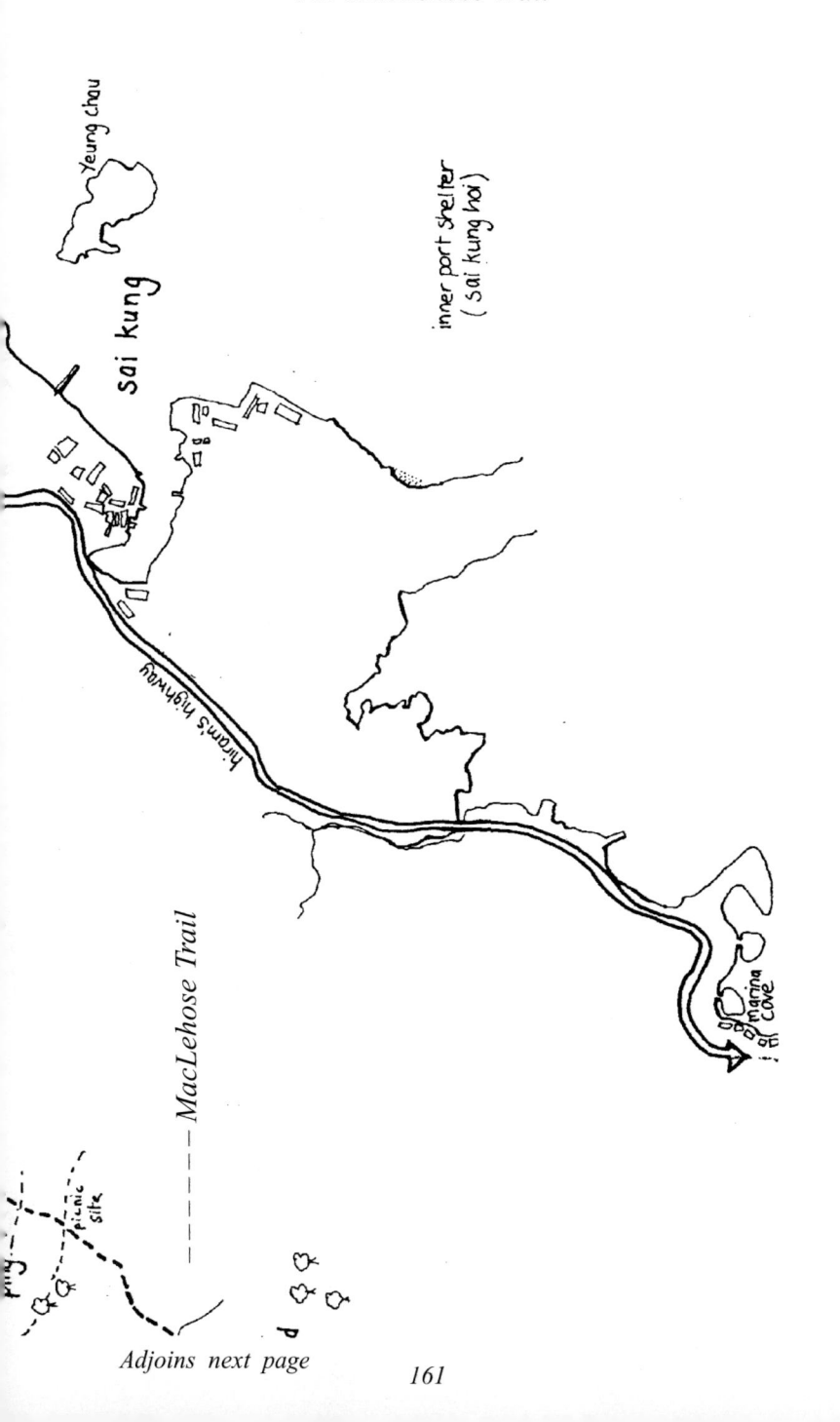

The MacLehose Trail

The MacLehose Trail

Adjoins Previous page

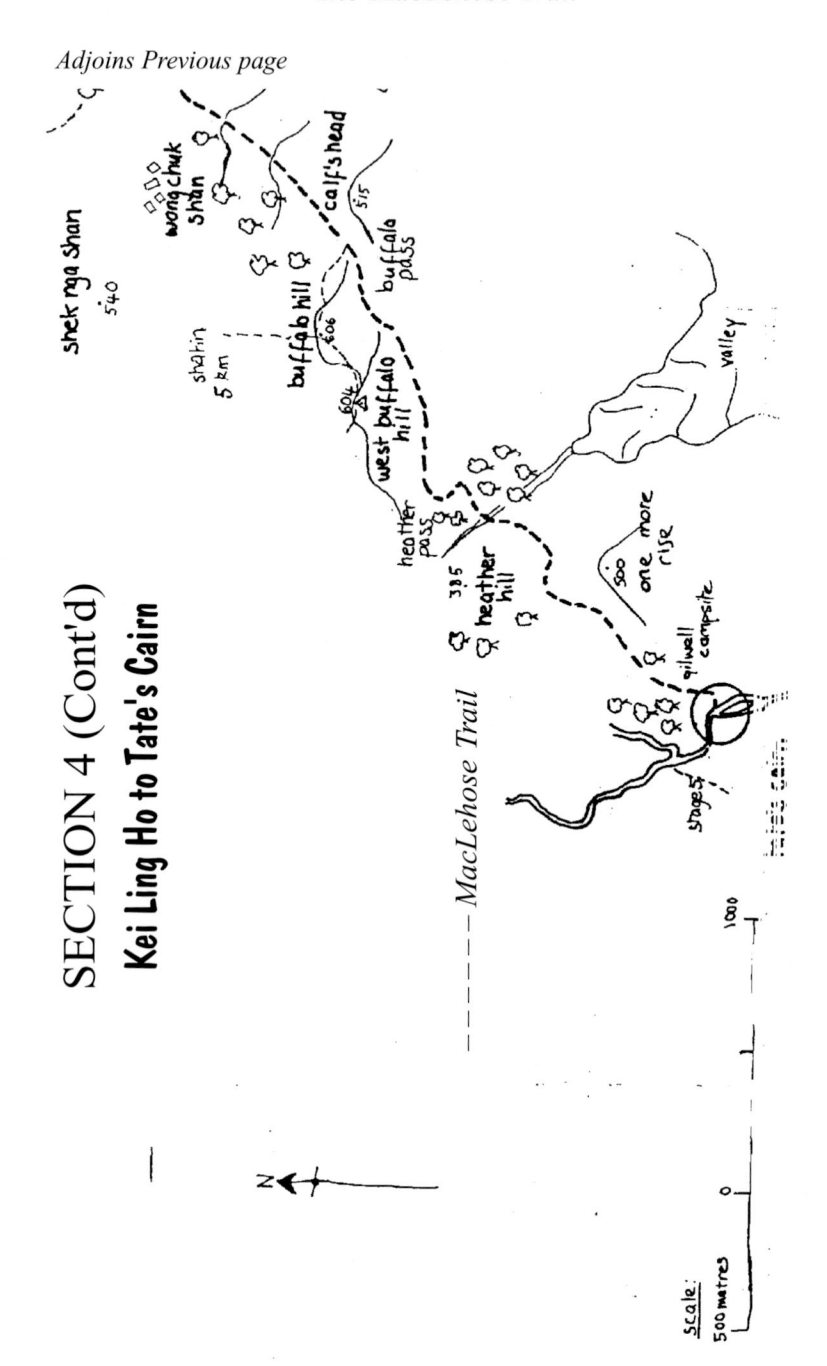

SECTION 4 (Cont'd)
Kei Ling Ho to Tate's Cairn

The MacLehose Trail

SECTION 5
Tate's Cairn to Tai Po Road
10.6 kilometres

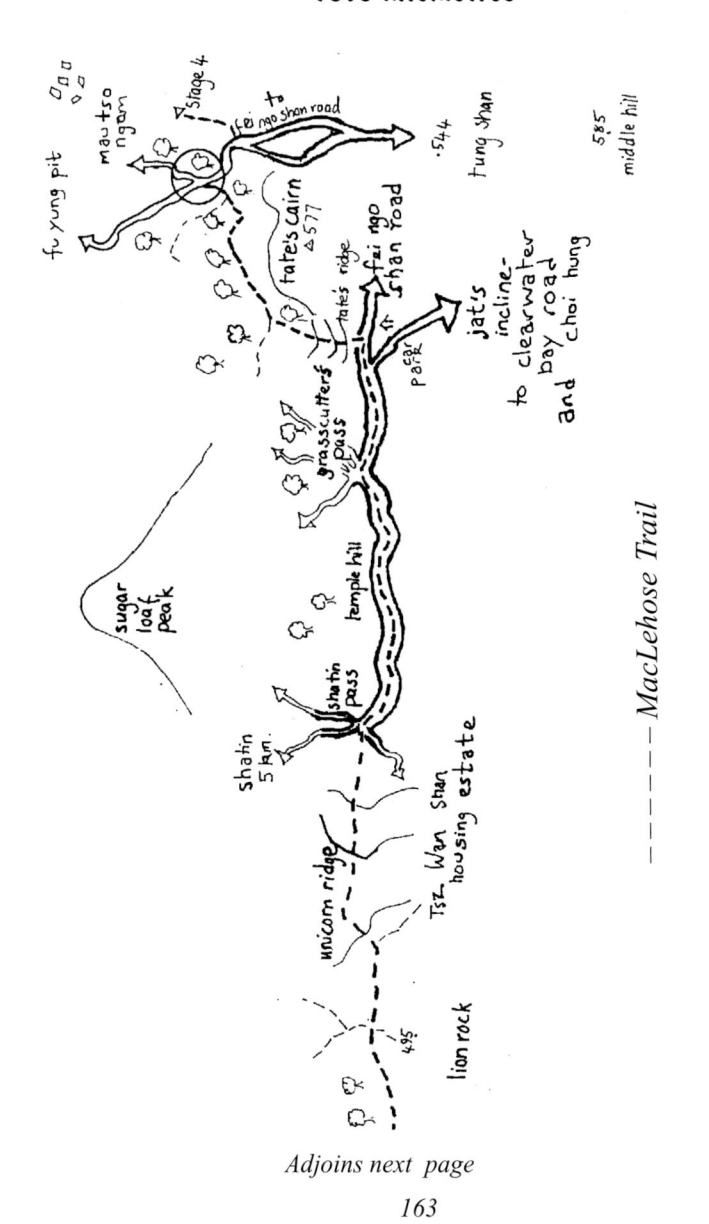

The MacLehose Trail

SECTION 5 (Cont'd)
Tate's Cairn to Tai Po Road

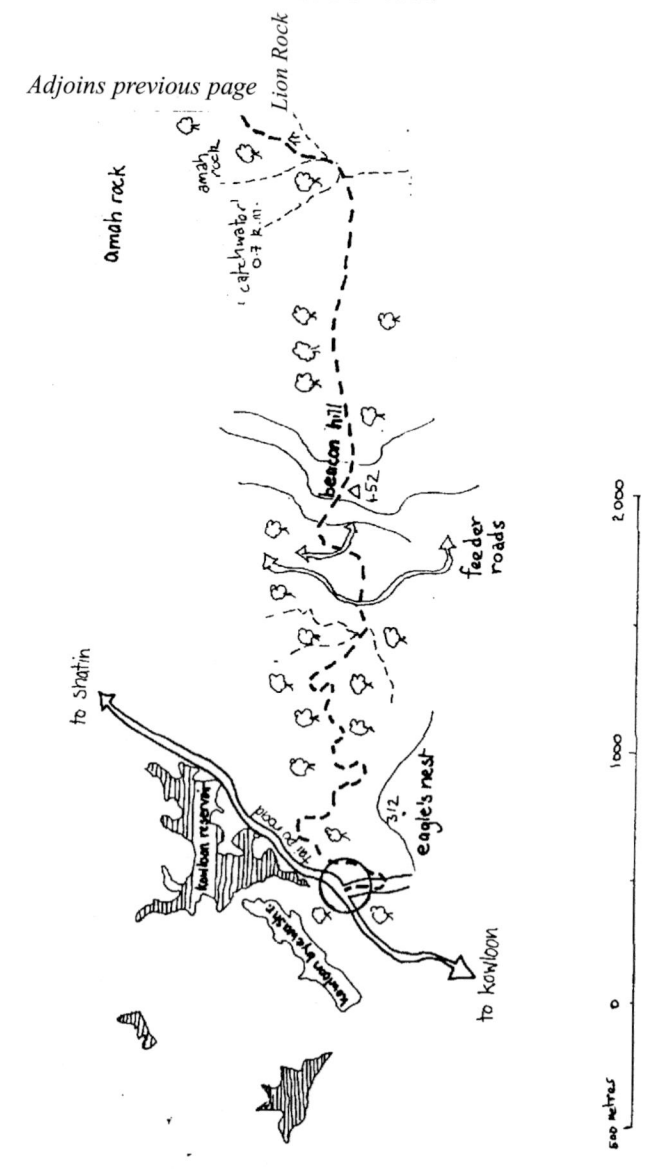

SECTION 6

Tai Po Road to Shing Mun Reservoir 4.6 kilometres

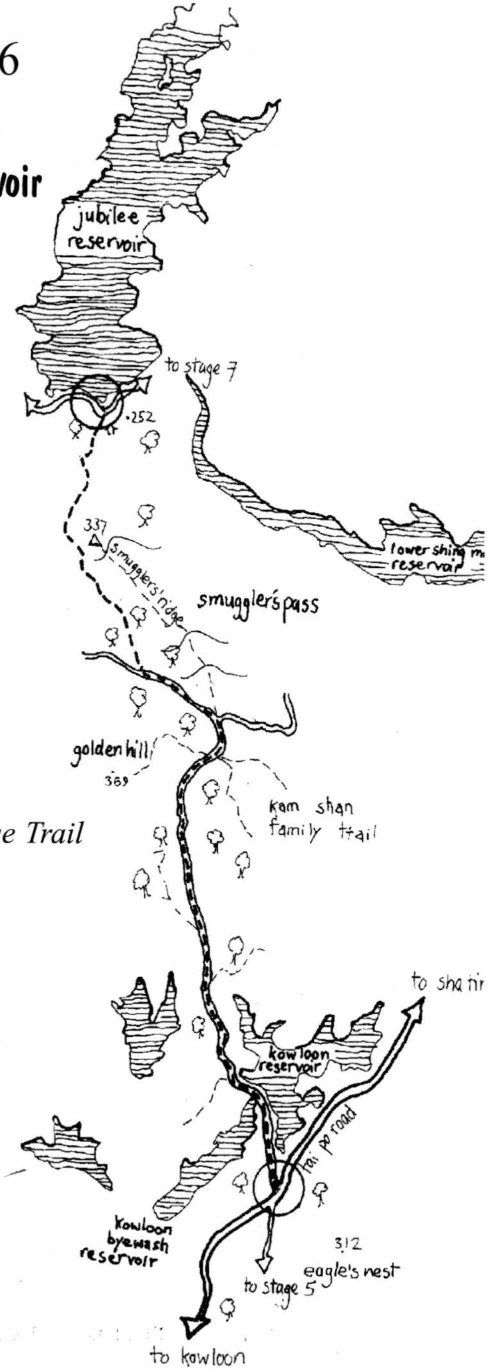

------ *MacLehose Trail*

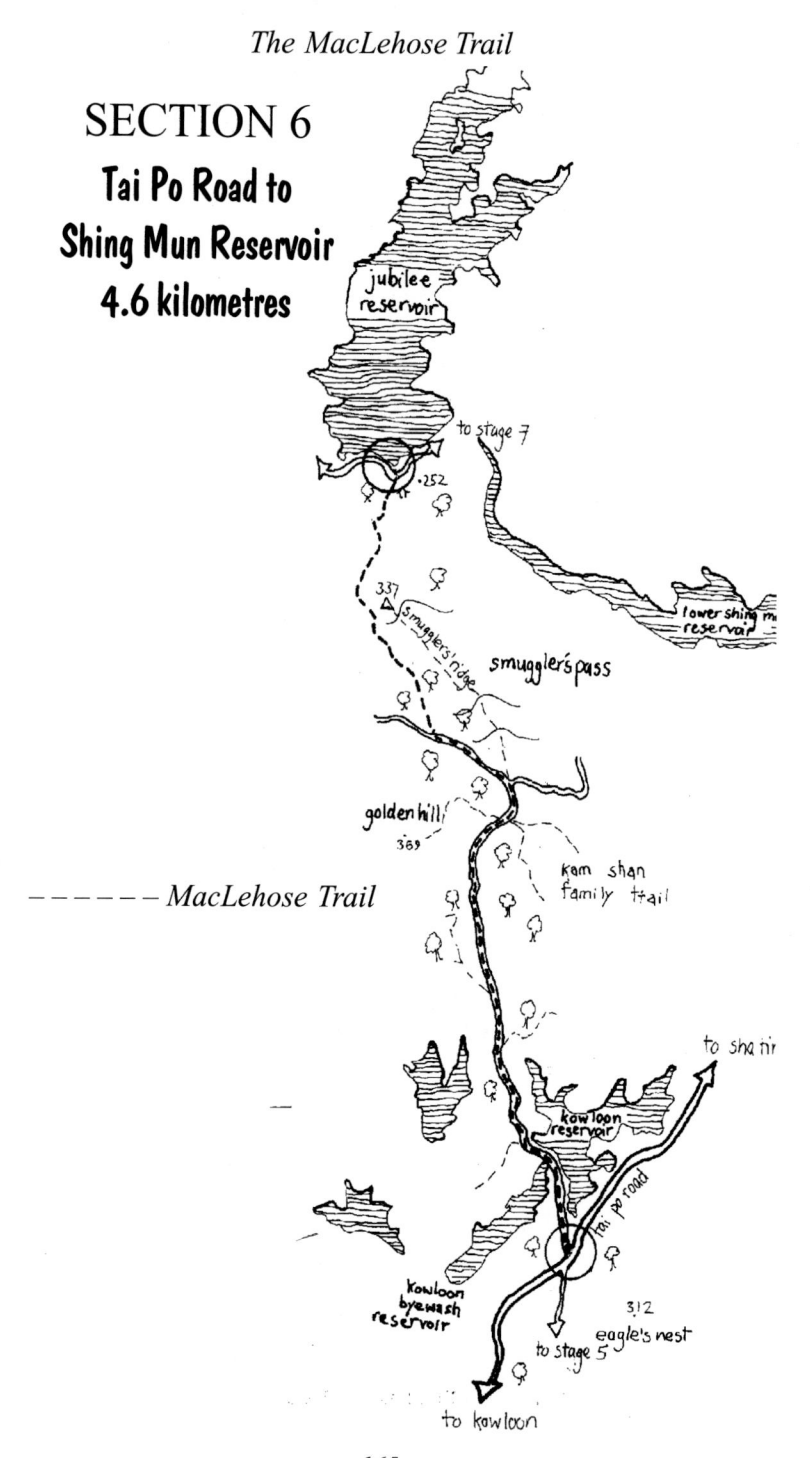

The MacLehose Trail

The MacLehose Trail

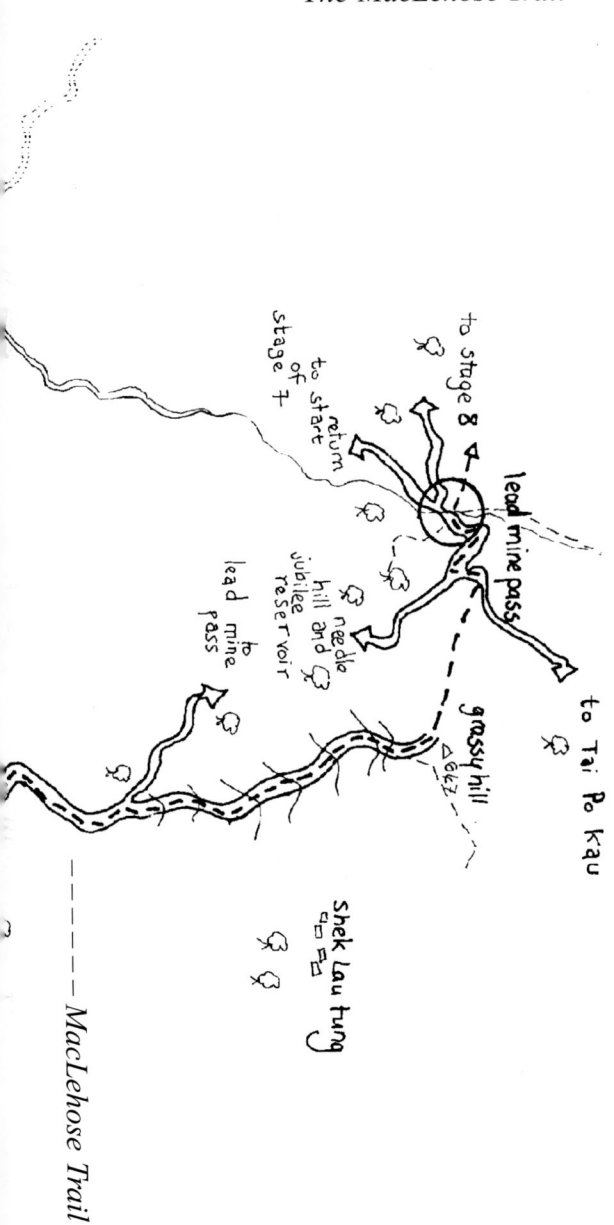

SECTION 7
Shing Mun Reservoir to Lead Mine Pass
6.2 kilometres

The MacLehose Trail

SECTION 8
Lead Mine Pass to Route Twisk
9.7 kilometres

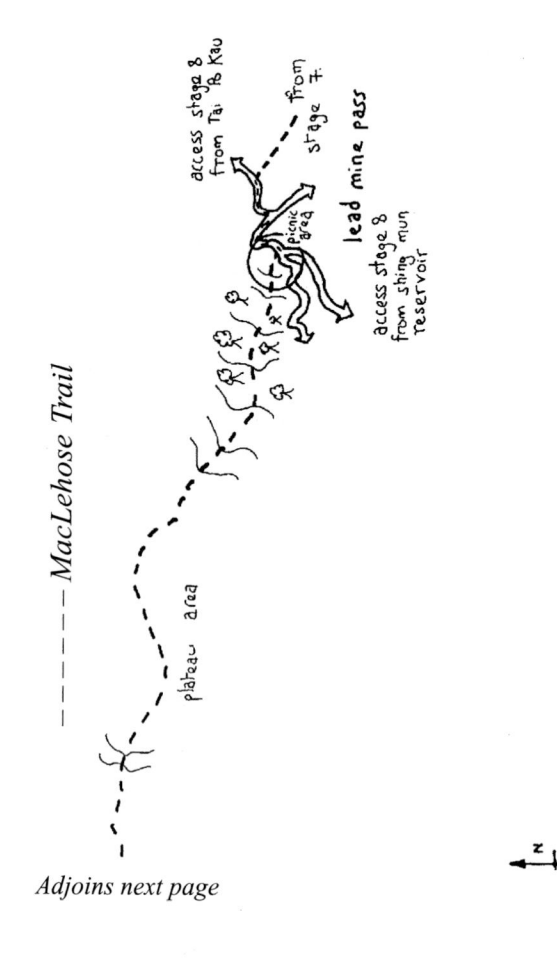

Adjoins next page

The MacLehose Trail

SECTION 8 (Cont'd)
Lead Mine Pass to Route Twisk

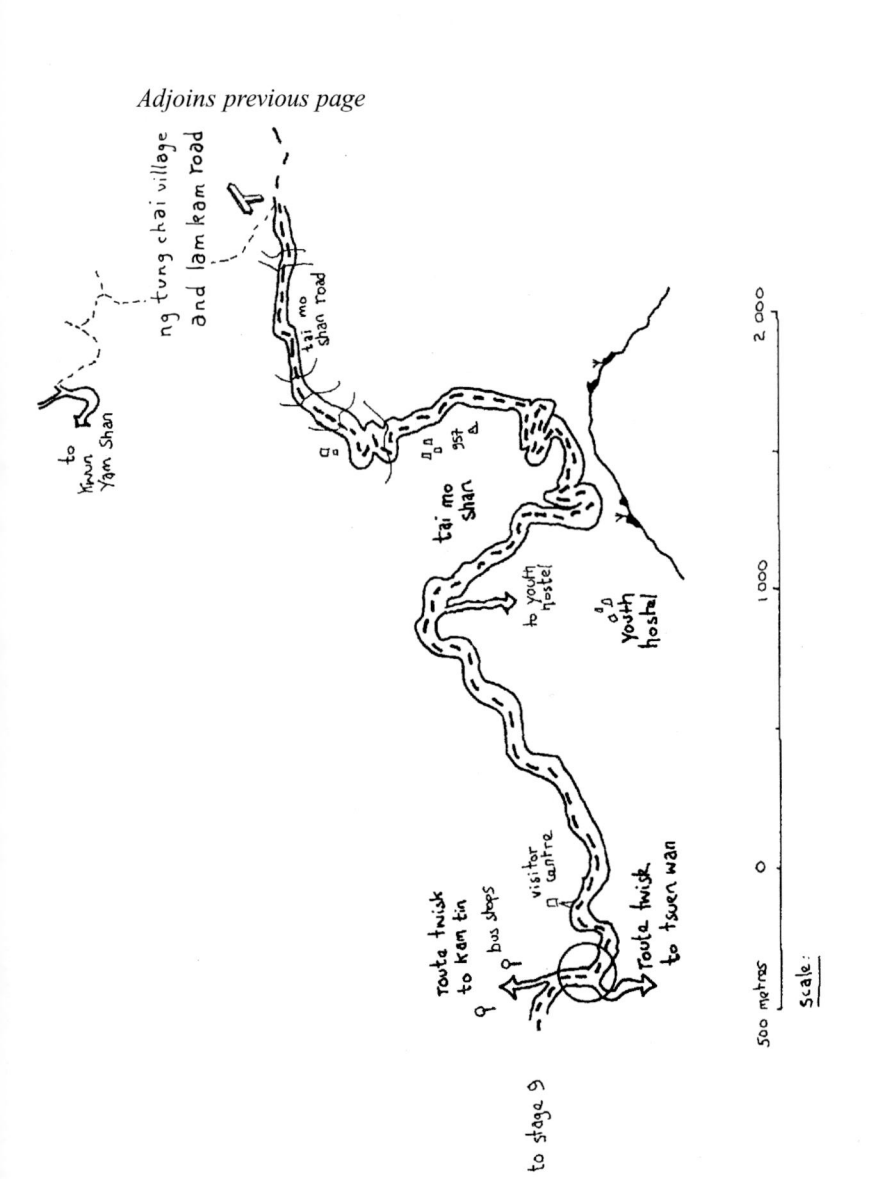

Adjoins previous page

The MacLehose Trail

SECTION 9(Cont'd)
Route Twisk to Tin Fu Tsai Campsite

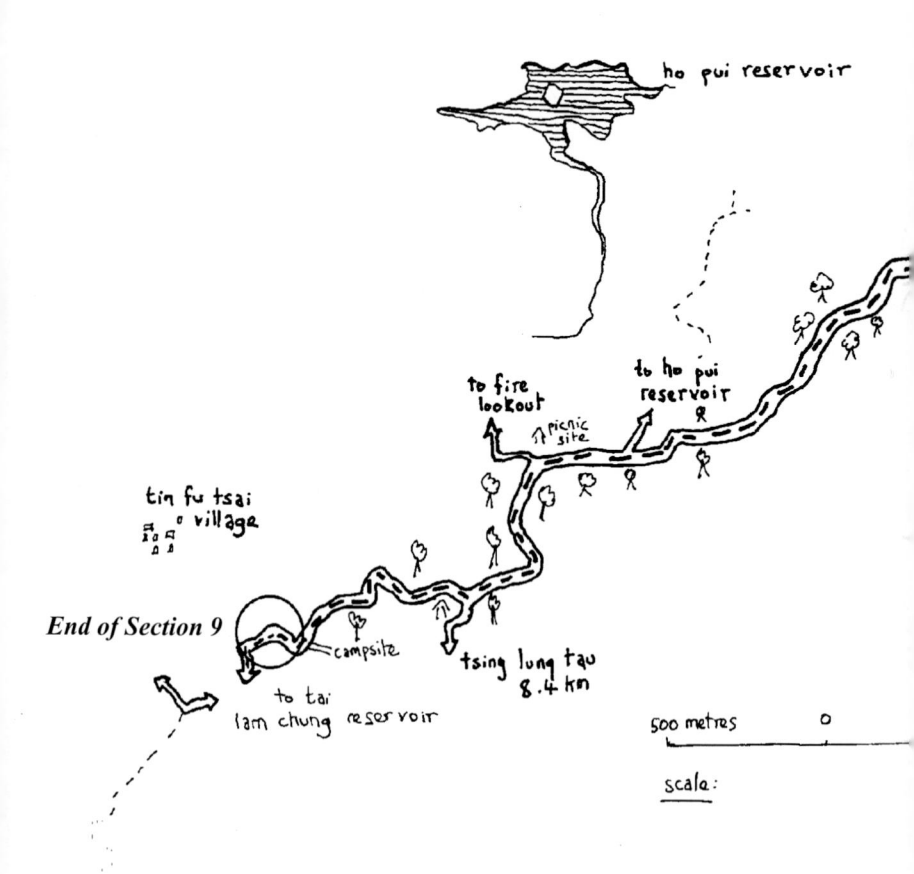

SECTION 9
Route Twisk to Tin Fu Tsai Campsite
6.3 kilometres

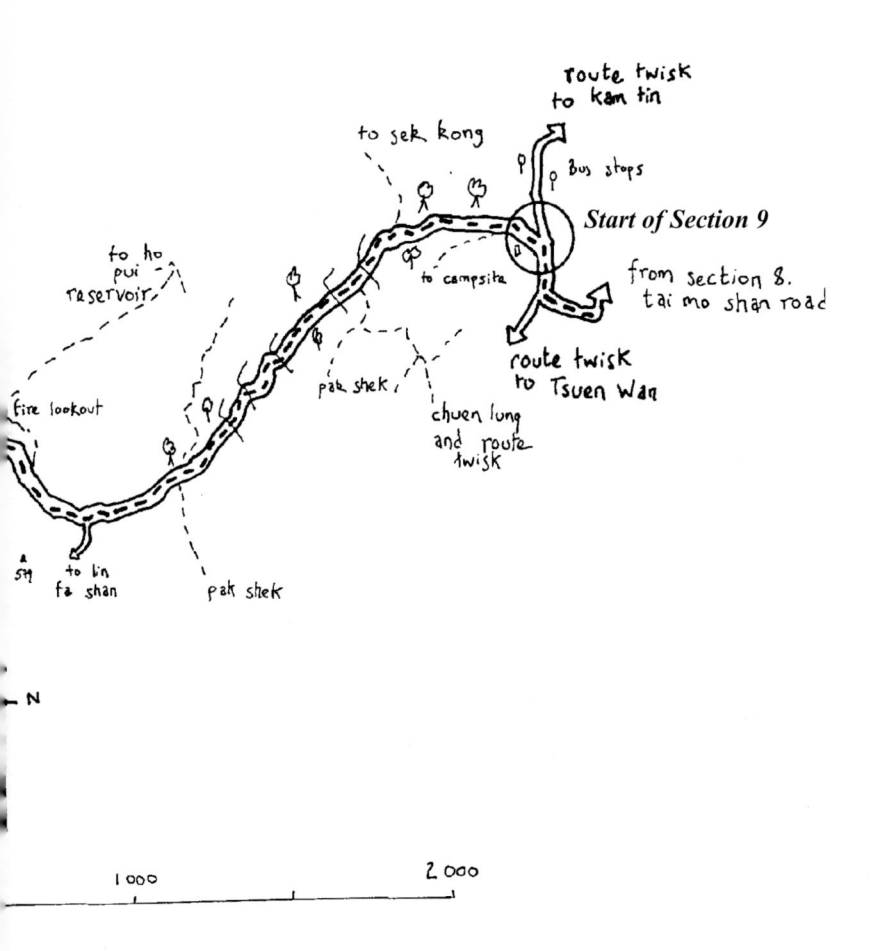

Start of Section 9

The MacLehose Trail

SECTION 10
Tin Fu Tsai to Tuen Mun
15.6 kilometres

Adjoins next page

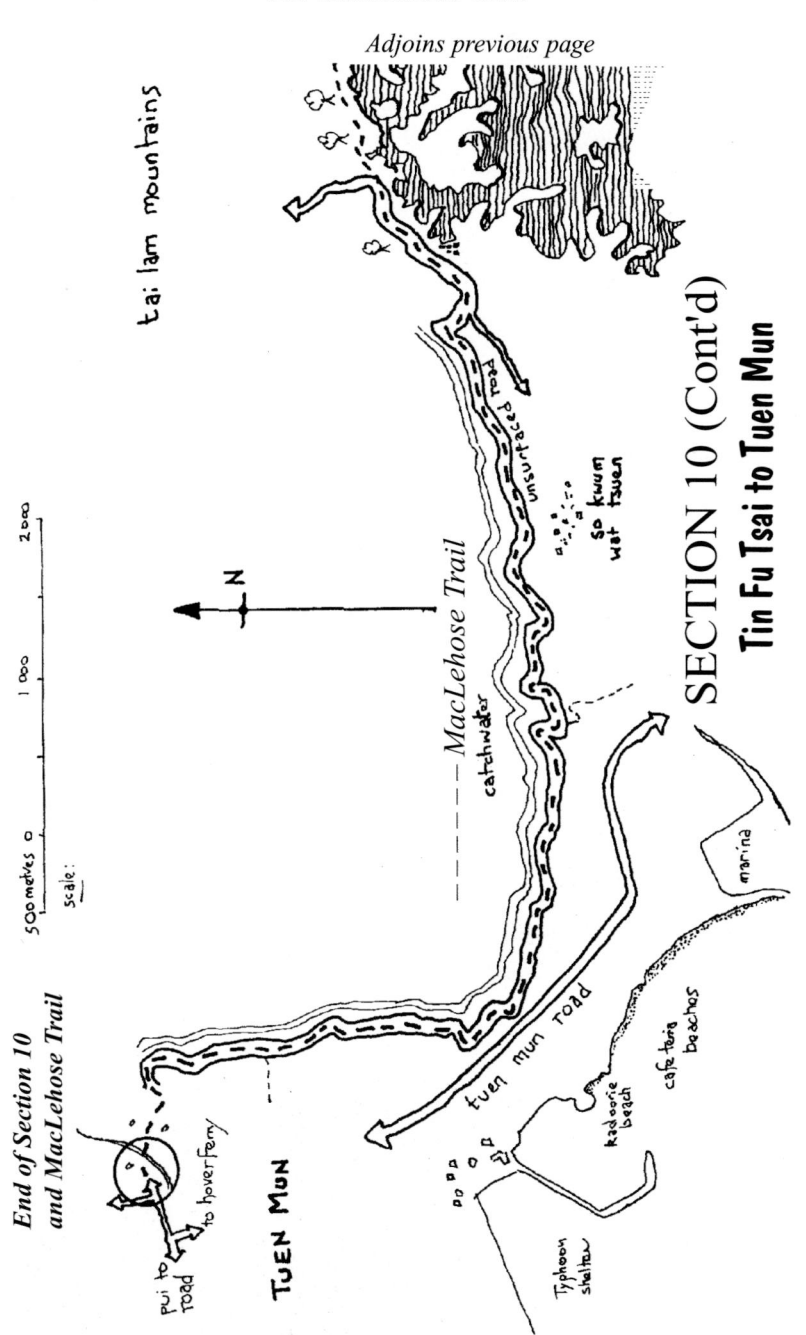

The MacLehose Trail

Adjoins previous page

SECTION 10 (Cont'd)
Tin Fu Tsai to Tuen Mun

The MacLehose Trail

Ko Lau Wan and half-way house (back).

Where the forest trail ends (near Cove Hill)

C. Excursions

The MacLehose Trail

△536 pyramid hill

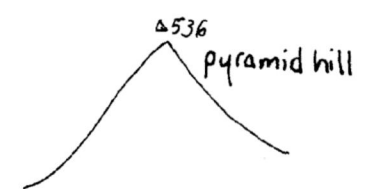

EXCURSION 1
Sai Kung to Shatin

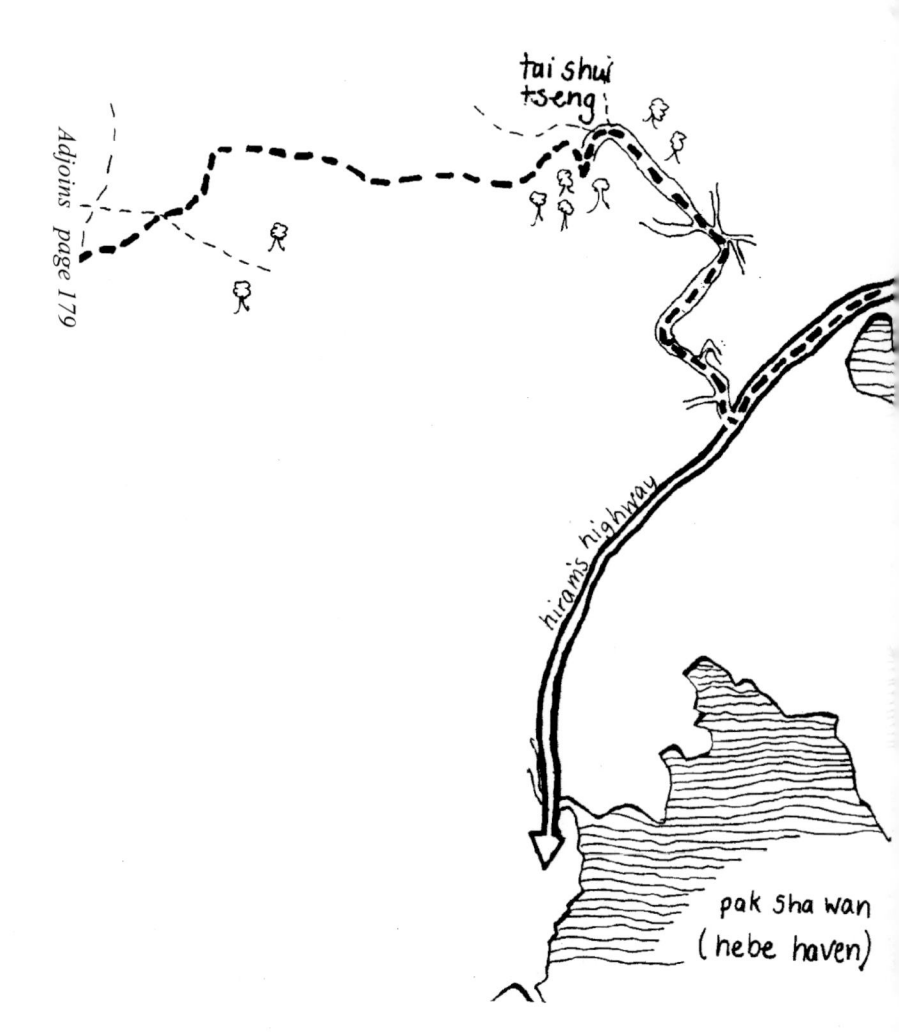

ngong ping

tai shui tseng

Adjoins page 179

hiram's highway

pak sha wan
(hebe haven)

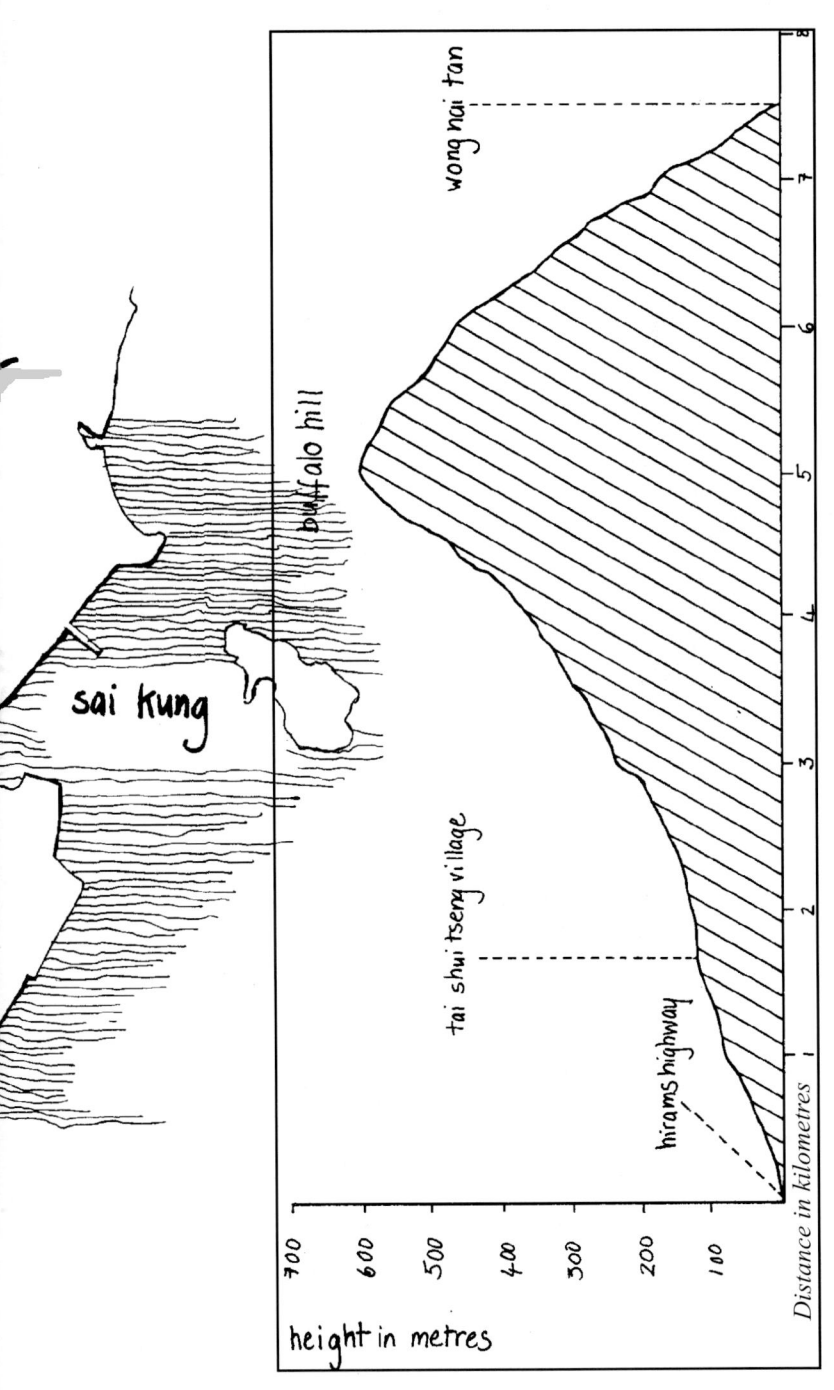

The MacLehose Trail

The MacLehose Trail

EXCURSION 1 (Cont'd)
Sai Kung to Shatin

nui po sh
(turret h

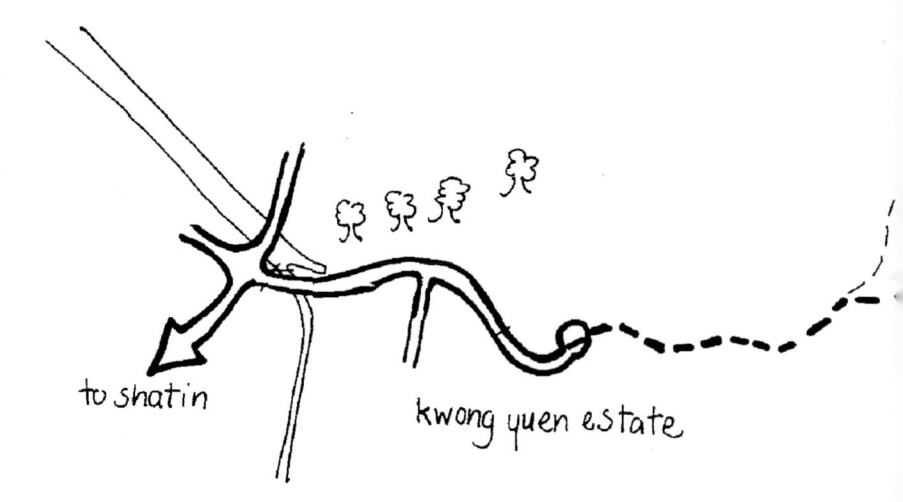

to shatin

kwong yuen estate

N

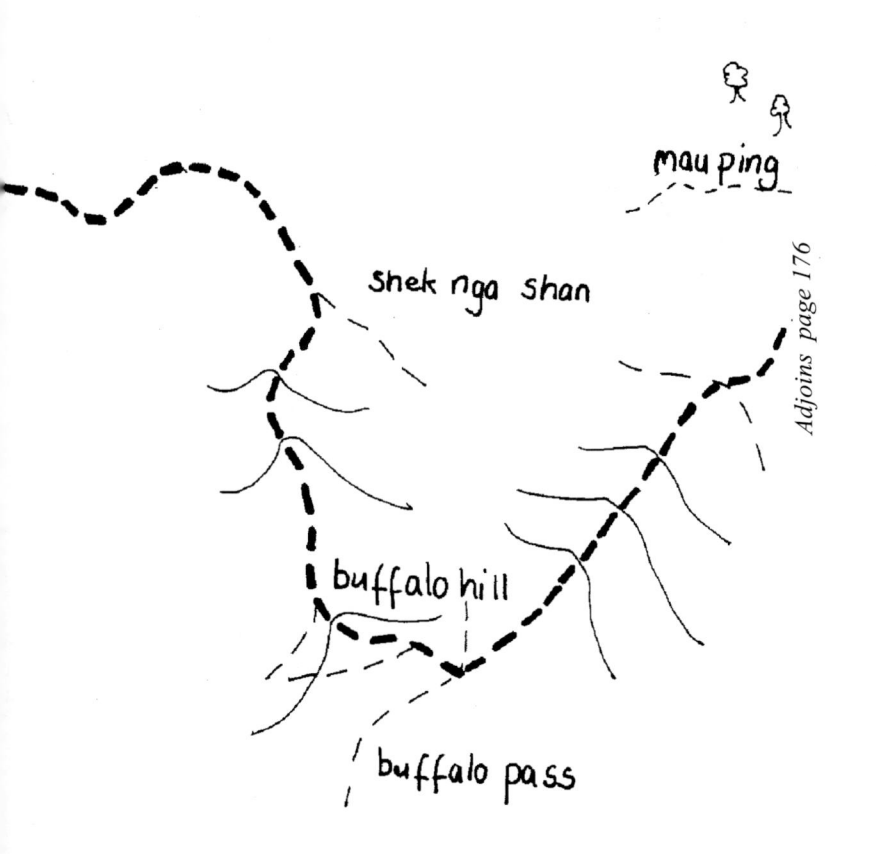

The MacLehose Trail

The MacLehose Trail

EXCURSION 2
Tai Wai to Tsuen Wan or Kwai Chung

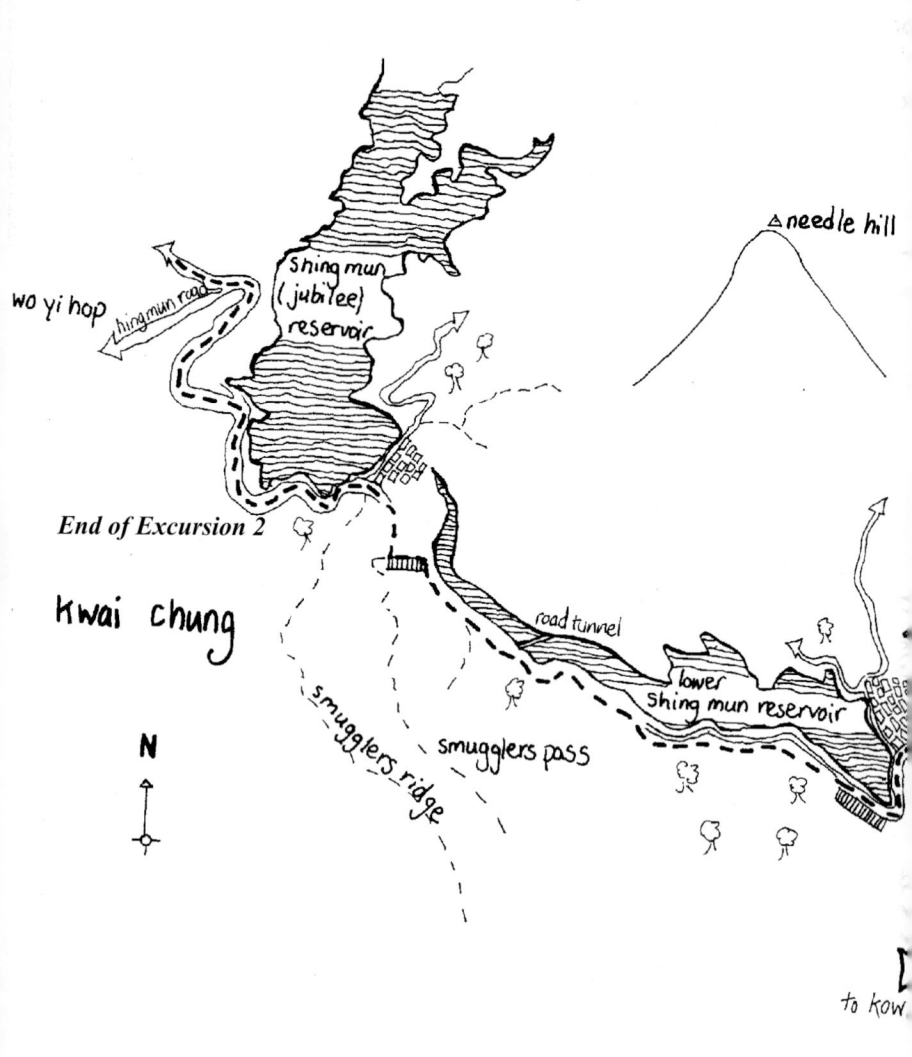

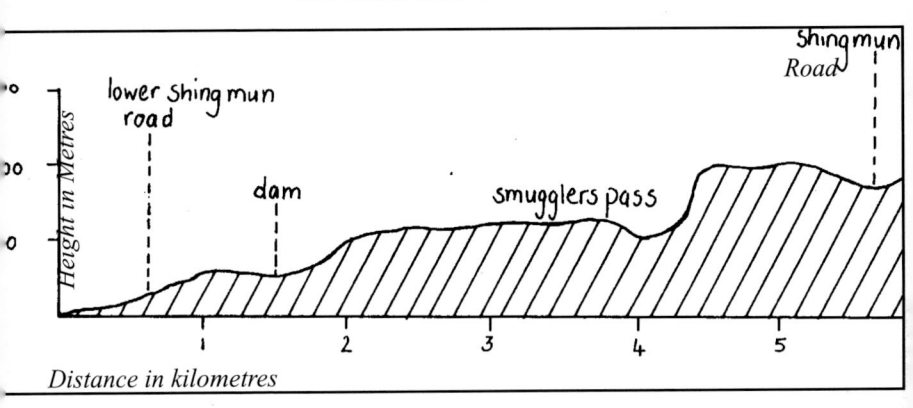

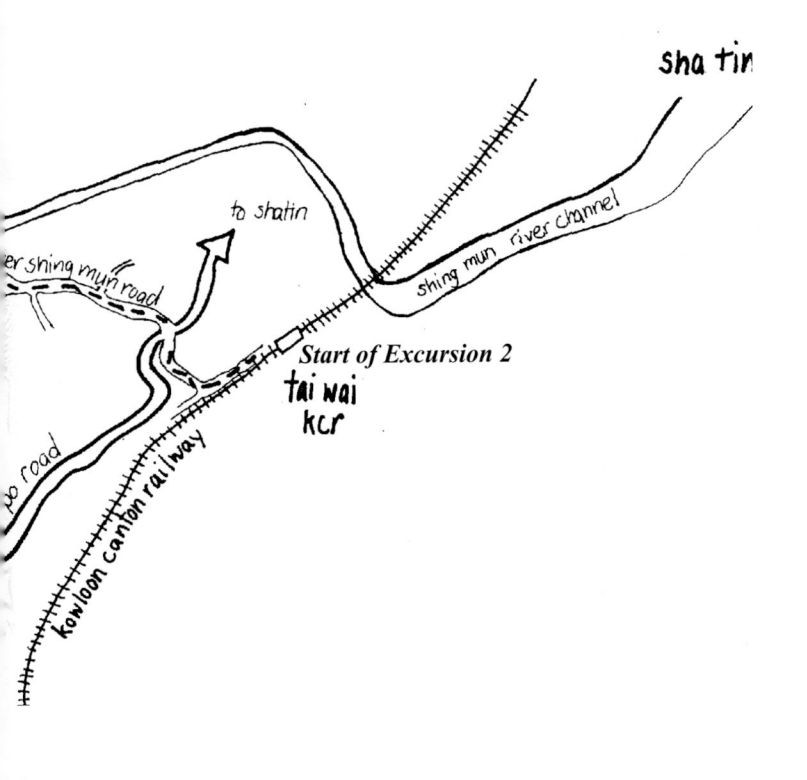

The MacLehose Trail

Height in Metres / Distance in kilometres

- lower shing mun road
- dam
- smugglers pass
- Shing mun Road

sha tin

to shatin

shing mun river channel

lower shing mun road

no road

kowloon canton railway

Start of Excursion 2

tai wai kcr

The MacLehose Trail

EXCURSION 3
Fo Tan to Grassy Hill

option 1

Adjoins page 184

④

option 2

cove hill
△399

③

option 1

fo tan kcr

Shatin Road

N

sha tin

to kowloon

The MacLehose Trail

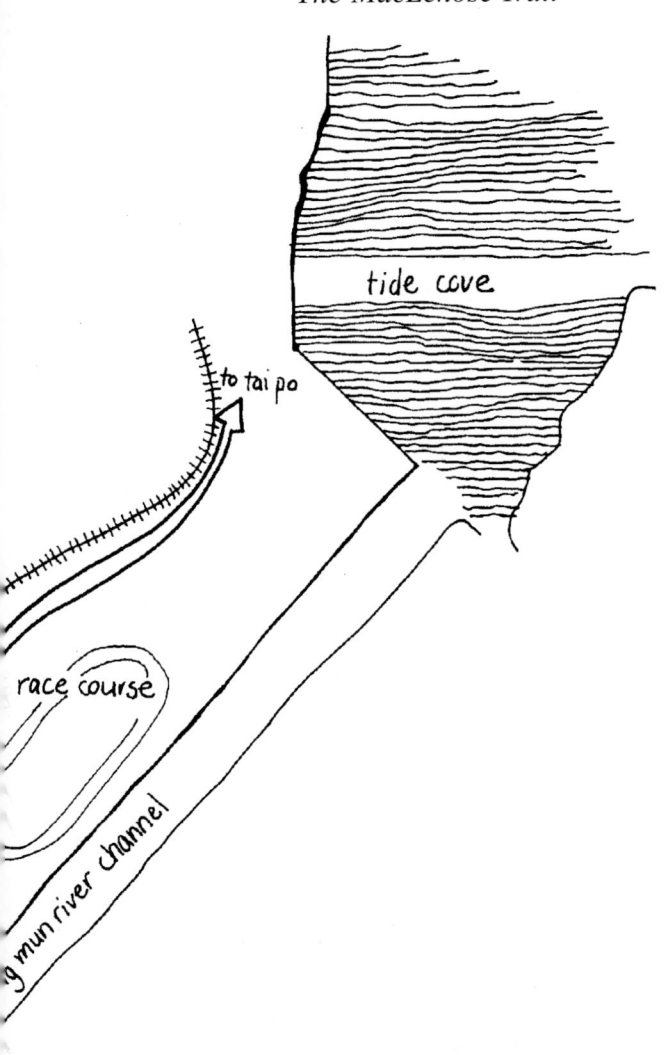

EXCURSION 3 (cont'd)
Fo Tan to Grassy Hill

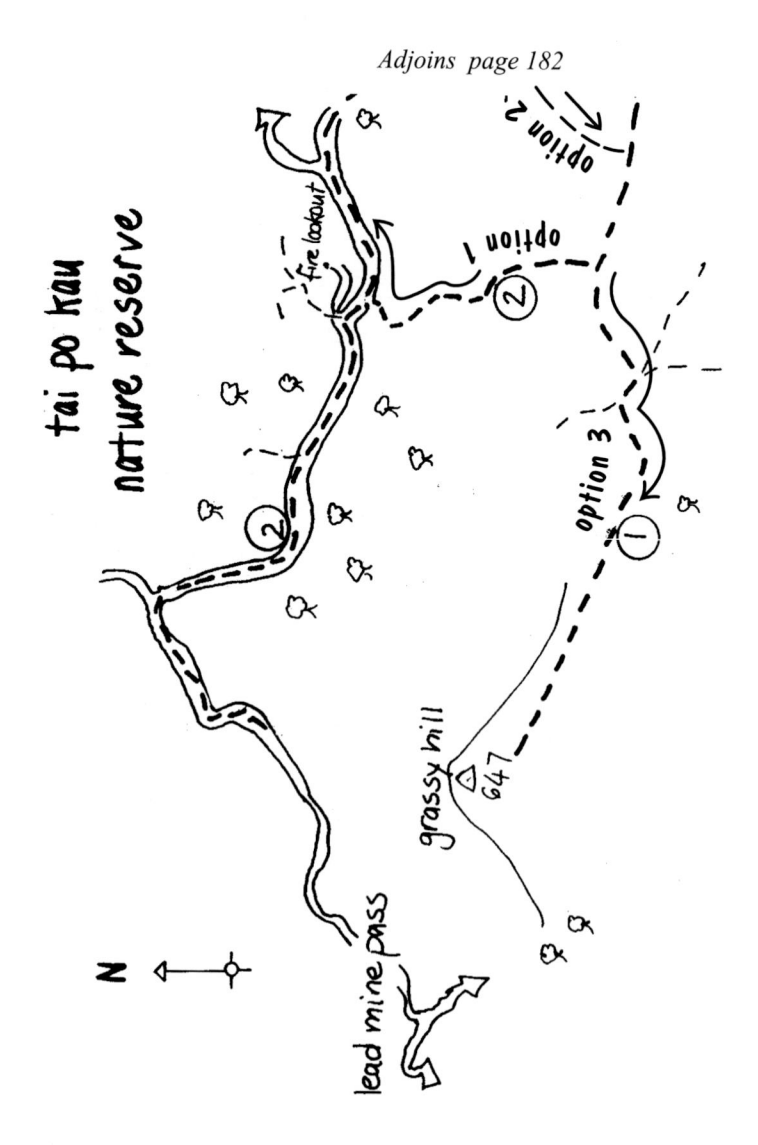

The MacLehose Trail

Excursion 3 :
a) option 1 (text) is diversion 4 (map)
b) option 3 (text) is diversion 1 (map)

diversion 1 to grassy hill
diversion 2 to lead mine pass
diversion 3 to tolo highway
diversion 4 to tolo highway

height in metres

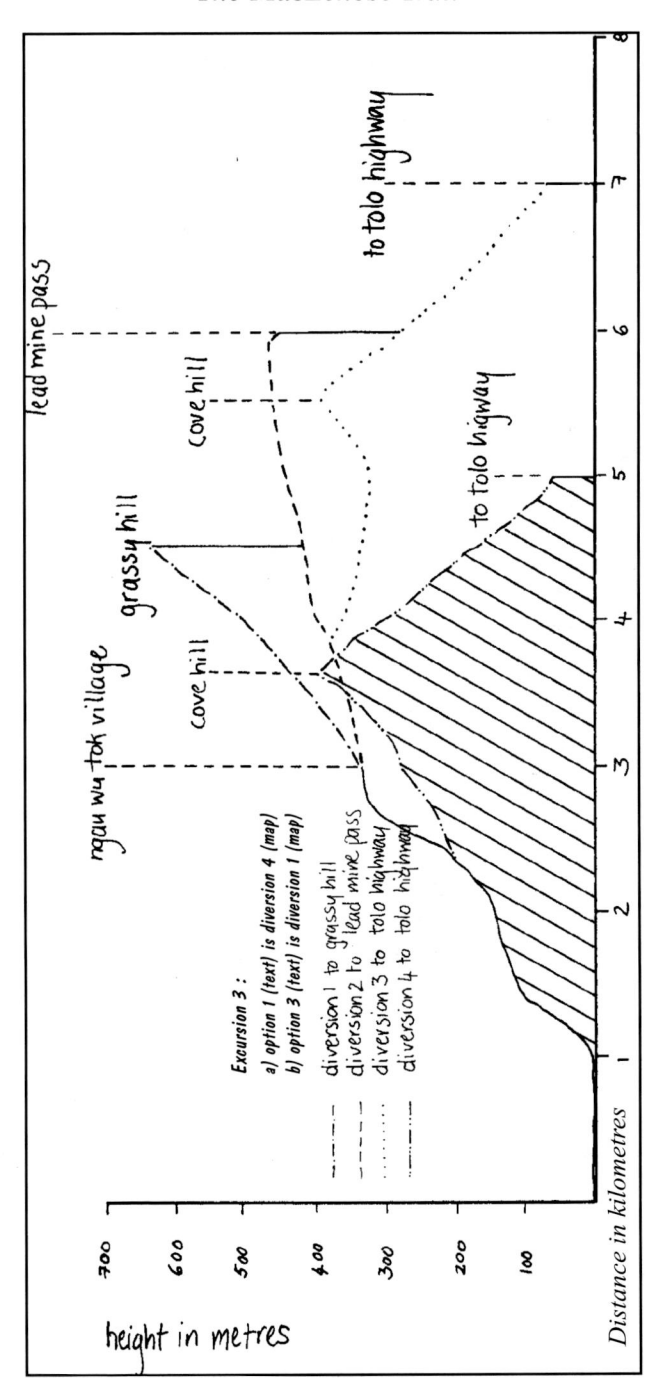

Distance in kilometres

The MacLehose Trail

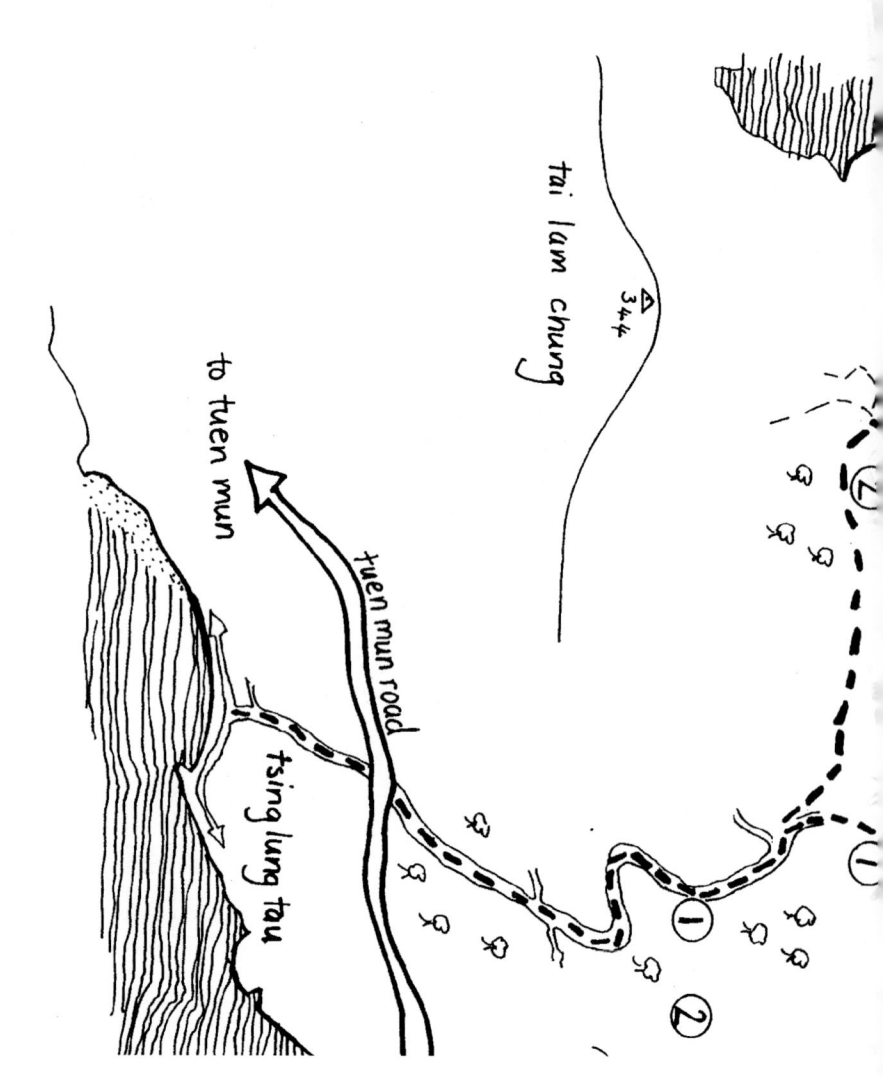

Adjoins page 188

The MacLehose Trail

EXCURSION 4
Tsing Lung Tau to Sham Tseng

tai lam chung reservoir

tai lam country park

Joins MacLehose Stage 10

joins page 188

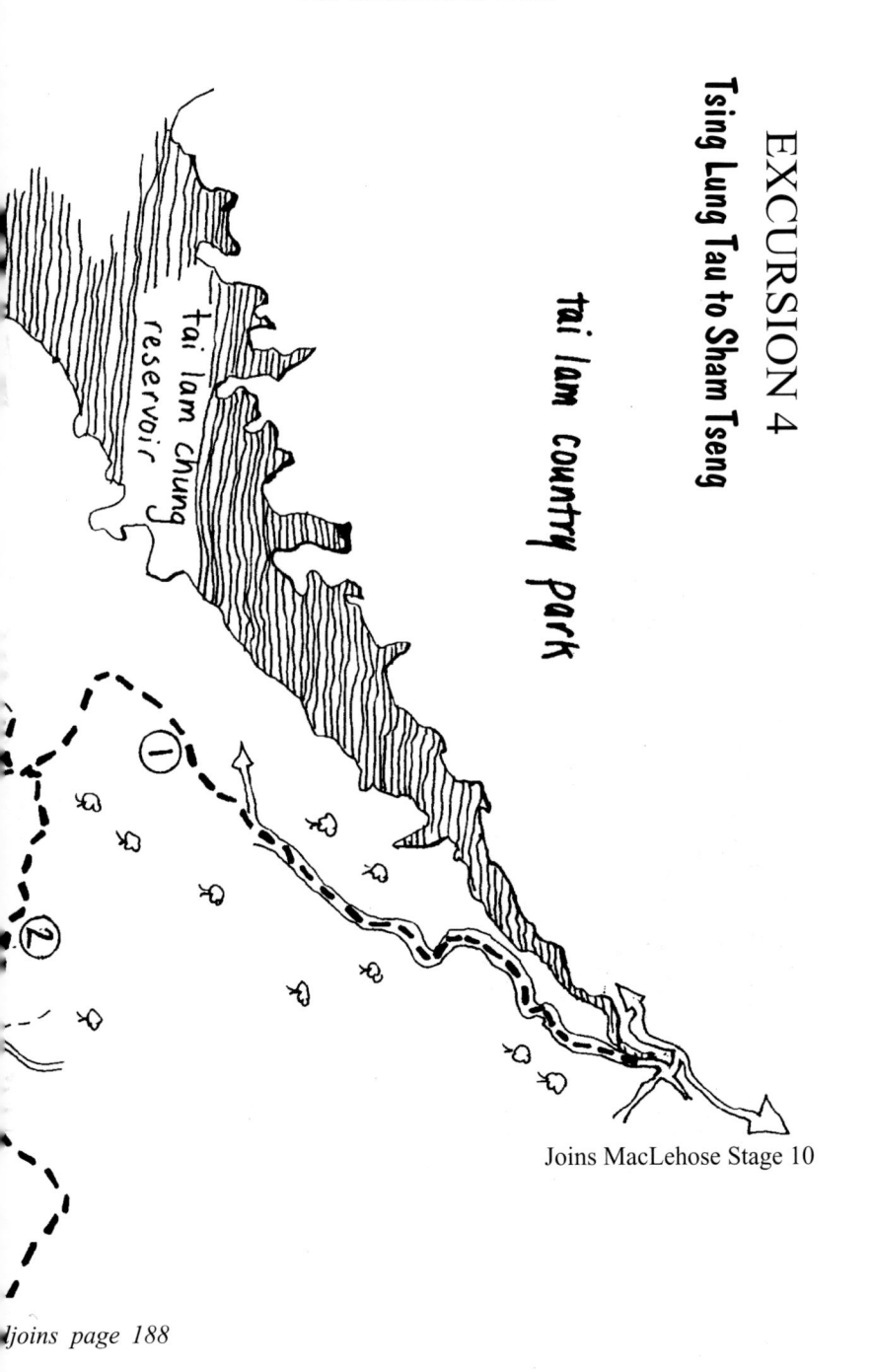

The MacLehose Trail

EXCURSION 4 (Cont'd)
Tsing Lung Tau to Sham Tseng

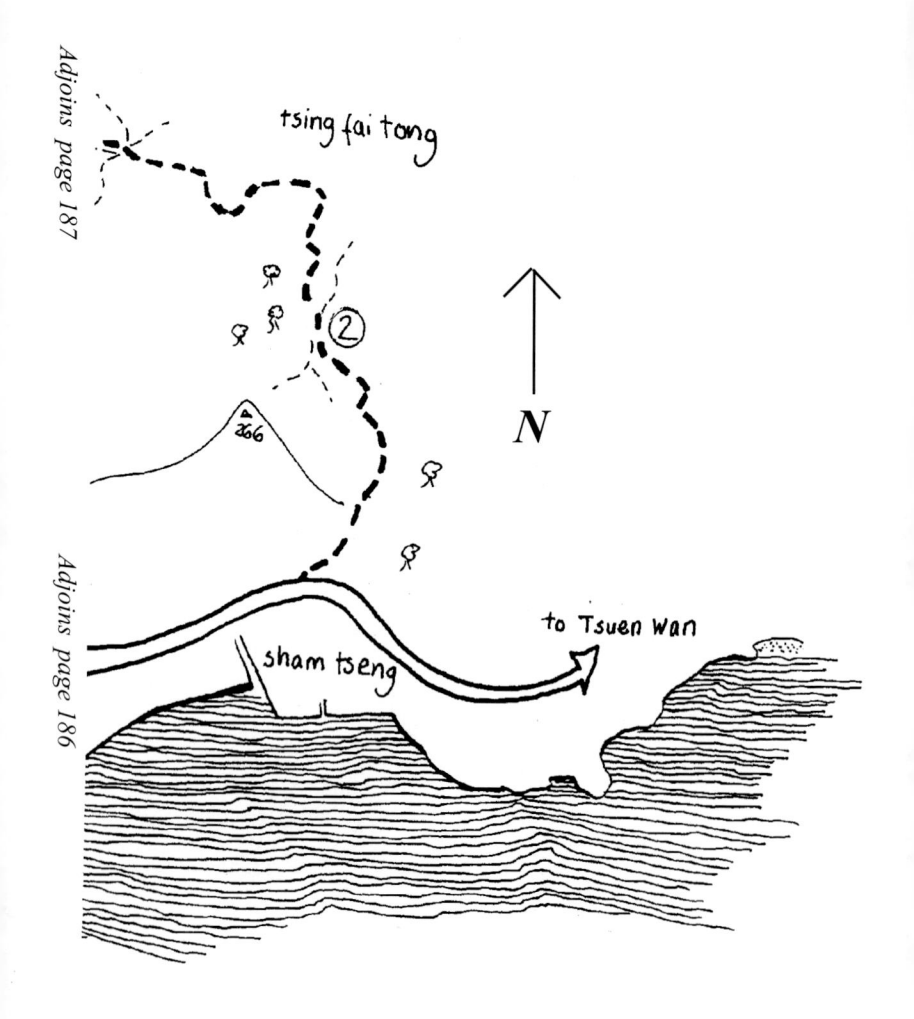

The MacLehose Trail

height in metres

key:
········· diversion 1 to join maclehose stage 10
– – – –   diversion 2 to sham tseng

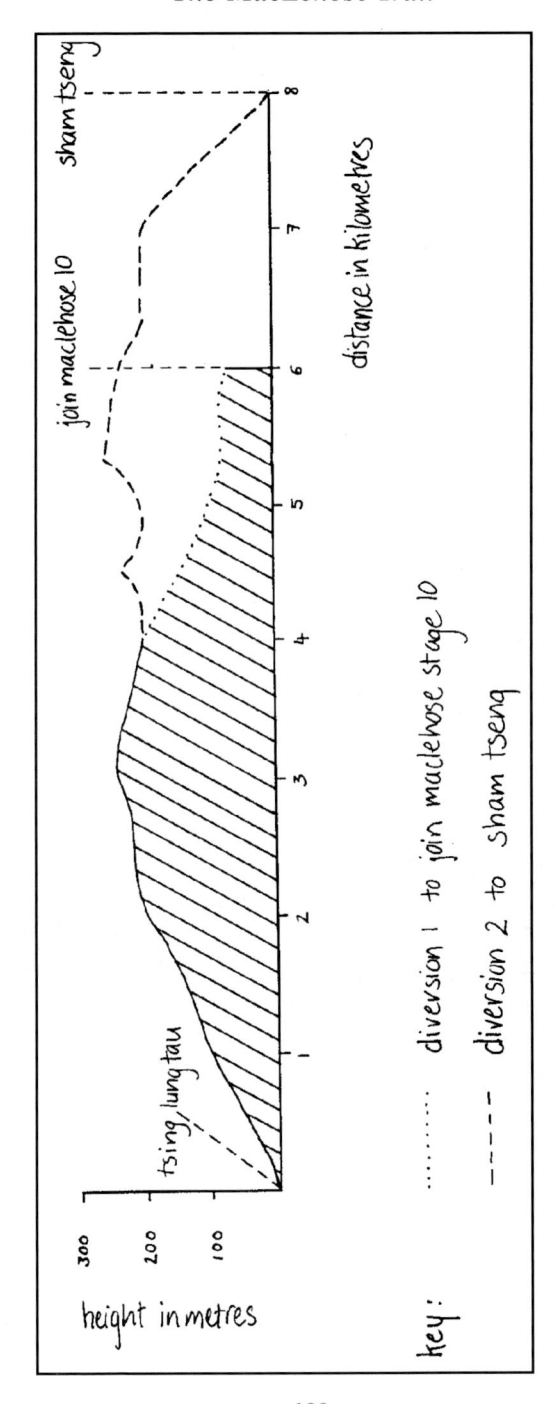

The MacLehose Trail

The following other books published by **The Alternative Press** are available in select bookshops in S.E. Asia but may also be ordered direct from the publisher. Prices include Seamail. If Registered Airmail is required, please add **US$2.50** per book (1-9; for Kalevala add US$6). US$ cheques on USA banks, US$ postal orders (all made out to "Kaarlo Schepel"), and bank drafts made on a Hong Kong bank made out to "The Alternative Press" are acceptable means of payment. Please allow 6 weeks for delivery of Seamail (outside Asia), 14 days for Airmail.

1) **The Solution** (256 pages) by **Karl Polak**. An explanation of emotional illness and diseases of alcoholism and drug addiction. Published in 2 editions, 1986 & 1987. **US$9.50**

2) **Magic Walks** (Vol 1) by **Kaarlo Schepel**. A Bestseller. Sixth Print in a reworked edition is due shortly. 20 Walks in Hong Kong's spectacular countryside 40% of which is country parks and hills. **US$8.00**

3) **Magic Walks** (Vol 2) by **Kaarlo Schepel**. Now replaced by Vol 2a (44 pages, 1992) and Vol 2b (96 pages, December 1994). 10 Walks each. **US$5.50** and **US$7.00** respectively.

4) **Magic Walks** (Vol 3) by **Kaarlo Schepel**. 68 pages including 16 pages in full colour. 10 Walks. **US$6.50**

5) **Restoring the Wholeness of Life** by **Dr Han Stiekema**. 94 pages. An alternative/complementary view of health, diet (vegetarian) and meditation. Published 1990. **US$7.50**

6) **Country Profit** by **Drs. C.J. de Koning**. 115 pages. Published 1989. (A few copies available). A banker's and economist's advice on how to solve the Third World's debt crisis. **US$11.00**

7) **Chinese Chess** by **Robert Lin**. 84 pages. An introduction into this intriguing game which has a lot in common with international chess. Published 1991. **US$10.50**

8) **Crash Course in Chess** by **Robert Lin & Kaarlo Schepel**. 84 pages. Published in 3 different editions. Second Print Hong Kong Edition: **US$5.50**

9) **Russian Handbook of Chess** by **GM Eduard Gufeld**. 250 pages. An encyclopaedia of openings. **US$13.00**

10) **The Kalevala** — The Finnish national epos in the Tamil language. 428 pages. Hardcover: **US$ 35.00** Softback: **US$19.00**

Appearing shortly! Eagerly awaited by the hiking fraternity in Hong Kong — *"The Wilson Trail"*